Inspirations for HISTORY

Published by Scholastic
Publications Ltd,
Villiers House,
Clarendon Avenue,
Leamington Spa,
Warwickshire CV32 5PR

© 1992 Scholastic Publications Ltd
Reprinted 1993

Written by David Bell
Edited by Juliet Gladston
Sub-edited by Jo Saxelby
Designed by Micky Pledge
Series designed by Juanita
Puddifoot
Illustrated by Catherine Ward
Cover design by Lynne Joesbury
Cover illustration by Caroline
Porter

Designed using Aldus Pagemaker
Processed by Pages Bureau,
Leamington Spa
Artwork by Liz Preece,
Castle Graphics, Kenilworth
Printed in Great Britain by
Ebenezer Baylis & Son, Worcester

British Library Cataloguing in Publication Data
A catalogue record for this book is available from the British Library.

ISBN 0-590-53018-6

CONTENTS

The author wishes to acknowledge
the assistance of Lynne Potter,
Advisory Teacher for Humanities,
Newcastle upon Tyne LEA and the
staff of the Education Library Service,
Newcastle upon Tyne LEA in the
compilation of Chapter 14, Resources
for teaching history.

INTRODUCTION

History

'Taken as a whole in four out of five of all the classes which studied history, the work was superficial. A factor contributing to this situation was undoubtedly a lack of planning in the work. Few schools had schemes of work in history, or teachers who were responsible for the planning and implementation of work in this field' (Primary Education in England, *DES [1978]*

HMSO). At the time when HMI wrote this report, primary history was in an uncertain state. Teachers often relied on outdated textbooks; topics and themes could be repeated twice or even three times in a child's school career and in some cases, teachers even doubted that history was an appropriate subject to be taught in the primary

school. All of that changed in the late 1980s and early 1990s with the introduction of the National Curriculum. History is now a foundation subject and children have an entitlement to be taught it from the age of five.

BACKGROUND

What is history?

History has a number of elements:
• the study of people, places and events and how they have related to each other through time;
• time, sequence and chronology;
• the study of evidence which allows judgements to be made about what actually happened in the past and in what order;
• the communication and evaluation of what has happened in the past and how this affects what is happening today.

Each of these four elements must be present if what is being done is to be recognised as 'history'. In that sense, it is a separate discipline or study distinct from, say, mathematics or science.

Why teach history?

Some people may answer the question, 'Why teach history?' by simply saying that they teach it because they have to by law. This, in itself, can never be a satisfactory answer, as the teaching that will result is likely to be sterile, arid and uninteresting. Others have the view that history is an irrelevance given the increasingly technological society in which we live. Those that hold such a view treat history as something like stamp collecting, interesting in its own right, but hardly the proper object of serious study by school children.

The working party which put together the National Curriculum for history was concerned that history should be seen in a wider context and gave a number of purposes for school history.
• *To help understand the present in the context of the past.* We live in a country and a world where problems and opportunities are a result of decisions made in the past; for example, would it really be possible to understand the turbulence of the Middle East without an understanding of both ancient and modern history?
• *To arouse interest in the past.* As there can be no absolute answers about the past, history raises questions and encourages children to speculate; for example, we might know when the Spanish Armada set sail for England, but what do we know about the motivation of the men who gave the order to sail? We can learn about how people made decisions in a variety of circumstances.
• *To help give children a sense of identity.* History is fundamental to knowing where you fit in a family structure. It allows children to understand from where they and their families came. More widely, they can begin to understand the position their community and country held in the world and what position they hold today.

We moved from Jamaica when your mum was only a baby....

• *To help to give children an understanding of their own cultural roots and shared inheritances.* British society is made up of people from a variety of backgrounds and cultures. The study of history helps children to learn about the richness of such backgrounds and how they have come together to create the interesting mix that is Britain today.

• *To contribute to children's knowledge and understanding of other countries and other cultures in the modern world.* The study of history allows children the opportunity to understand how other peoples and societies have changed and developed over time. The study of history, and an awareness of the rich history of others, helps to counteract prejudice and insularity.

• *To train the mind by means of disciplined study.* History brings together skills such as analysis, argument, the recognition of patterns and presenting points of view.

• *To introduce children to the distinctive methodology of historians.* History is a form of study in its own right. As part of a general education, children should be introduced to the methodology of the historian and seek to exercise such skills themselves.

• *To enrich other areas of the curriculum.* History helps children to understand the evolution of mathematical and scientific ideas, as well as the ways in which art, music and literature have developed over time.

• *To prepare children for adult life.* History helps children as they grow to adulthood to understand the nature of the society in which they are taking their places.

In some ways, such arguments can be criticised as being idealistic and not exclusive to history alone. However, it is these aims as a whole that make history unique and worthy of an important place in the school curriculum.

The history of history teaching

In the latter part of the nineteenth and the early part of the twentieth centuries, the teaching of history had a moral purpose. The book, *Suggestions for the Consideration of Teachers and Others Concerned in the Work of Public Elementary Schools*,

published in 1905 and quoted in Joan Blyth's book *History in Primary Schools* (Open University Press, 1988), recommended teaching history so that children learned their rights and duties, as well as understanding the vital role that Britain had played in developing virtue worldwide! Even as late as the 1920s, the Board of Education guidance on the teaching of history was still emphasising its role in encouraging good citizenship.

The practice of elementary teachers changed little from this early view and right up to the second World War the emphasis was placed firmly on learning dates and kings and queens. Training colleges did not consider history to be a very important subject and thus young teachers were often thrown back on their own devices once in the classroom. Indeed, even after the Second World War and throughout the 1950s, history teaching was often seen as no more than the telling of a few

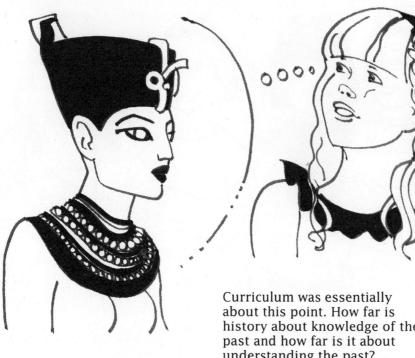

good stories. By the late 1950s and early 1960s, there was some emphasis on chronology and time-lines, but the turning point did not come, as with much else in primary education, until the mid 1960s with the publication of the Plowden Report (*Children and their Primary Schools* [1967] HMSO). In itself, the report said little of interest about history. However, by placing greater emphasis on topic work and integrated teaching, this report affected primary history substantially. Many teachers realised that here was a way of teaching history that was much more appropriate to the needs of younger children.

Nevertheless, by the time HMI reported on primary education in 1978, it was clear that the increased emphasis on topic work had meant that some basic skills and knowledge of primary history were not being taught. In a sense, the controversy that surrounded the introduction of history in the National

Curriculum was essentially about this point. How far is history about knowledge of the past and how far is it about understanding the past?

The central elements of teaching history

Although the National Curriculum prescribes both the content and outcomes of children's learning in history, there is still considerable discretion open to teachers in planning and organising their work. However, there are a number of central principles that underpin the teaching and learning of history.
• Careful planning needs to be done if children are to undertake a rigorous and coherent programme of study in history.
• There needs to be a reasonable balance between learning historical facts and acquiring historical skills.
• Both the teaching and learning of history can be enlivened by the use of a range of teaching styles and methods, for example whole class lessons, small group discussions and individual research.

• Chronology and the understanding of the place of events and people in time is an important aim of history.
• There has to be considerable emphasis on people, both great and humble, in order to bring history alive.
• As far as possible, children should be introduced to artefacts and evidence relevant to the period they are studying.
• Children should be given the opportunity to imagine what it was like to live in another period.
• There needs to be an awareness of both the content and methods of history teaching at later stages, particularly the early years of secondary education.

Although these include some general principles, a number of comments need to be made about both younger and older primary-aged children.

Four- to seven-year-olds
Prior to the introduction of the National Curriculum, the teaching of history was practically non-existent for this age group. This often reflected the very real concern that history was not an appropriate study for very young children. In particular, teachers were concerned that the long and applied periods of study necessary to understand a historical period were inappropriate. On the

other hand, topics such as 'The Romans' or 'The Egyptians' were often undertaken and although they were enjoyed by the children, it was sometimes difficult to see what contribution such projects were making to the development of children's historical understanding.

There is a danger of underestimating young children. It *is* possible to start developing historical understanding in children of this age particularly if it is developed from a position which is familiar to them; for example, the family, the school, visits to old sites and so on. Firsthand experience of historical artefacts will assist young children to begin to make judgements based on evidence and develop an idea of simple chronology.

Seven- to eleven-year-olds

Perhaps one of the most significant failures of the topic-based approach to primary history was that it failed to recognise children's natural and developing curiosity to behave like historians. Just as children learn the simple disciplines of science and technology, so they should be encouraged to learn the disciplines of the historian, for example, the rigorous analysis of evidence and the making of judgements based on information from a variety of sources.

History in the National Curriculum

The National Curriculum in history has two major components: attainment targets (and associated statements of attainment) and programmes of study.

There are three attainment targets in history, all of which overlap.
• Attainment Target 1: Knowledge and understanding of history – this attainment target is essentially concerned with historical change and continuity. In addition, it looks at the causes and consequences of key events and periods in history, and asks children to know about and understand the key features of such events and periods.
• Attainment Target 2: Interpretations of history – this attainment target is concerned with the way in which we interpret the past. Children are encouraged to see that there are different interpretations of the past which can vary and even contradict each other for many reasons. It also gives children the opportunity to examine a range of interpretations of the past including those from the period concerned and those which have been formed over time.
• Attainment Target 3: The use of historical sources – this attainment target is concerned with the key elements of history as a discipline. Children are encouraged to use historical sources and judge their reliability as sources after careful analysis and interpretation.

Essentially the programmes of study are designed to enable children to develop knowledge and understanding of British, European and world history. The programmes of study at Key Stage 1 and Key Stage 2 have four main components:
• key elements, which are intended to summarise the major themes of the programme of study and describe some of the ways in which they can be taught;
• links with attainment targets,

which describe how the historical content and knowledge can be related to the demands of the attainment targets;
• historical enquiry and communication, which describe how children should learn and communicate their findings about the past through oral, useful and aesthetic means;
• study units, which at Key Stage 1 is one unit in which children can develop an awareness of the past, while at Key Stage 2, they consist of both core and supplementary units.

Understanding the relationship between the attainment targets and the programmes of study is critical to an understanding of the National Curriculum for history. Children can only achieve the attainment targets through studying the historical content of the programmes of study. Within the National Curriculum document the links with attainment targets are described for each programme of study. This reinforces the links between the end product of the attainment targets and the content and process of programmes of study.

History at Key Stage 1
At Key Stage 1, there is only one core study unit. In it, children are encouraged to develop an awareness of the past and how it is different from the present.

Initially, the children can learn about the past through myths and legends, stories and eyewitness accounts. Firsthand experience will also be important and any or all of the following will be useful:
• historical artefacts;
• pictures and photographs;
• music;
• old buildings and sites.

Young children will learn best if activities are set in contexts that are familiar to them such as the family, home, shops and so on. This will allow them to move into the past with ease. In particular, children in Key Stage 1 should investigate:
• changes in their own lives and those of their families or adults around them;
• changes in the way of life of British people since the Second World War;
• the way of life of people in a period of the past beyond living memory.

Famous events or themes such as Christmas and anniversaries provide other opportunities for historical study.

History at Key Stage 2
The history curriculum for Key Stage 2 is broken down into core and supplementary study units. These cover major developments in British history, although there are also opportunities for children to study local history, historical themes and the history of other civilisations. Due regard should be paid to chronology both within a theme and between themes. The core study units are:
• CSU1: Invaders and settlers: Romans, Anglo-Saxons and Vikings in Britain;
• CSU2: Tudor and Stuart times;
• CSU3: Victorian Britain;
• CSU4: Britain since 1930;
• CSU5: Ancient Greece;
• CSU6: Exploration and encounters 1450 to 1550.

Children are required to study CSUs 1, 2, 5 and 6 and one or both of 3 and 4.

The supplementary study units are:
• A: a unit involving the study of a theme over a long period of time (at least 1,000 years), chosen from:
– Ships and seafarers;
– Food and farming;
– Houses and places of worship;
– Writing and printing;
– Land transport;
– Domestic life, families and childhood.
• B: a unit based on local history.
• C: a unit involving the study of a past, non-European society chosen from:
– Ancient Egypt;
– Mesopotamia;
– Assyria;
– The Indus Valley;
– The Maya;
– Benin.

Children are required to study three or four units, which should include at least one unit from each of the categories A, B and C.

Planning to teach National Curriculum history

At first sight the two key stages to be taught at primary school appear to be the extremes of teaching history. Key Stage 1 appears to offer almost total freedom over content in the context of some quite general attainment targets, while Key Stage 2 is much more prescriptive.

Therefore, the history curriculum requires careful thought and planning in order to ensure that the following requirements are met.
• Children must have access to all the compulsory elements of National Curriculum history over their years at primary school.
• Teachers must balance out the amount of history taught both within a year and between years in order to ensure that neither they nor the children are overloaded or bored.
• There must be a balance between history which is taught as a discrete subject and history which forms part of wider topics encompassing a range of other National Curriculum subjects.

Who plans?

Few schools will have the staff available to give one person responsibility for history alone. It is likely that history will form part of a wider responsibility for the humanities which could encompass history, geography and religious education. It is far too much to expect such a person to, on his or her own, plan out the history curriculum for the whole school. It is more likely that such a person will co-ordinate the work of teams of people to look at different areas, such as Key Stage 1 or lower Key Stage 2. Whatever plans emerge, it is likely that the school will wish to revise its curriculum plan in the light of experience. For example, a school will have to evaluate how far history should become a discrete subject in the upper primary school. This in turn may be determined by the aptitude and ability of the children.

However, a history co-ordinator can have a number of key roles. She or he can:
• co-ordinate the work of individuals and teams and,

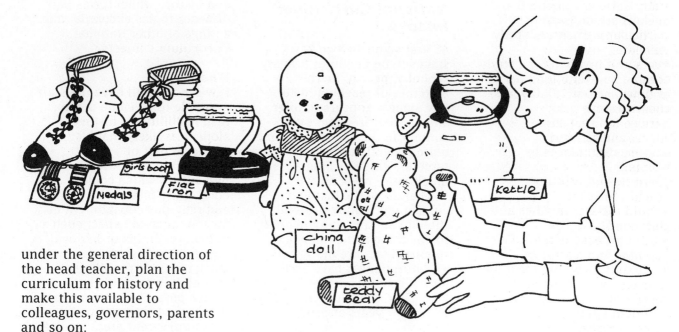

under the general direction of the head teacher, plan the curriculum for history and make this available to colleagues, governors, parents and so on;
• evaluate the approach the school has to history and, in particular, consider whether the balance of activities is correct both within a year group and between year groups;
• co-ordinate the assembly, management and distribution of topic and subject packs to be used by teachers year by year;
• keep an up-to-date list of books and resources available for both teachers and pupils and provide suggestions for new purchases as money becomes available;
• establish, if one does not already exist, a collection of artefacts collection including items such as newspapers, clothes, household objects, coins and so on. In addition, she could act as the school archivist for registers and so on;
• arrange occasional history events for parents and others, including exhibitions of work, role plays, performances and so on;

• keep governors and others involved and informed, through written documentation and verbal presentations, on the progress of history within the school;
• provide advice to colleagues on all aspects of history teaching including planning, lesson suggestions, classroom management and assessment;
• act as a link person with outside specialists and agencies such as LEA advisers and professional associations such as the Historical Association.

The history curriculum plan
The National Curriculum Council's *Non-statutory Guidance for History* suggests that schools need to develop a curriculum plan for each key stage or phase for which they are responsible. This plan should include:
• aims and objectives;
• the order in which study units should be taught;
• curriculum plans for each year group;

• provision for pupils at different levels of attainment, including those with special educational needs;
• links with other subjects and cross-curricular elements, including equal opportunities;
• resources to be used;
• teaching methods;
• methods of assessment and record-keeping;
• a scheme of work for each study unit;
• arrangements for monitoring and review.
   All of this may seem a very demanding task for a primary school, especially given that it has a number of other plans to implement and subjects to teach in a National Curriculum format. However, the important point to make is that such a plan does not need to be completed all at once. The broad structure should be in place so that teachers have a general idea of what needs to

be taught in any particular year. However, the details, such as schemes of work for particular units, may be developed over a number of years as the curriculum is formally introduced. Such a plan will also help the school identify some priorities for in-service training and may identify books and resources that need to be purchased.

It is important to stress that there is no 'right' plan for teaching history. Schools should make their own decisions based on:
• their general approach to teaching and learning;
• the extent to which the curriculum is organised into discrete subjects or taught in an integrated manner;
• the experience of the staff in teaching history;
• the amount of time allocated to the teaching of history.

History as a discrete element
This approach, which is more appropriate to Key Stage 1, would essentially see the teaching and learning of history as a discrete element within the curriculum. It is unlikely, however, that the children would see it in the same way as they might see maths or writing, in that there are unlikely to be discrete history lessons in the same way that there would be individual maths or writing sessions. Units such as 'All about me', 'Fact and fiction', 'Lives of famous people' and so on, could be taught as 'one-off' lessons or, over a longer period of time, as history mini-topics.

Clearly, there will often be an overlap of topics between the two/three year groups of Key Stage 1 (Reception, Year 1 and Year 2). Additionally, teachers will need to ensure that their lesson content is appropriate to meet the needs of the statements of attainment at the different levels.

History through integrated topics
This approach would put the teaching and learning of history in Key Stage 1 within the context of wider topics, also incorporating for example geography, science, technology, English and maths. Topics could include 'Houses and homes', 'Journeys' and 'Festivals'. In some ways, more careful planning is required if this approach is used, in order to ensure that the history element takes its proper place and the children are given appropriate opportunities to meet the statements of attainment at the different levels.

In reality, most Key Stage 1 teachers are likely to combine elements from both approaches, teaching history through integrated topics, but incorporating some one-off lessons or mini-topics around local or national events or around visits and visitors to the school.

Chronological teaching
For Key Stage 2 it is a very good idea to teach the British core units in chronological order, although it is not a requirement. This will help the children to progress more easily to Key Stage 3, where there is a requirement to teach certain core units in chronological order.

Such an approach, however, is not without its difficulties, as pupils may not be ready for the concepts associated with a particular study unit. For example, 'Tudors and Stuarts' has traditionally been taught at the upper end of the primary range because it has been felt that children are more able to appreciate the details of this period by this age. By the same token, it could be argued that a topic on 'Britain since 1930' allows younger children to begin from their own experiences and those of their families. Also, a chronological approach may not allow for the best links to be made between supplementary units. Children are likely to benefit more from being taught in a sequence which intersperses units of different types. In primary schools that are organised with mixed-age classes it is also difficult to organise the teaching of history chronologically, even though it is possible to construct the curriculum as a cycle of study units; the length of the cycle depending on the number of age groups in a class.

If a school chooses not to teach the core study units in a chronological way, it is then left with the problem of ensuring that children are introduced to the concept of chronology. This can be achieved, to a degree, by using time-lines to show where one unit fits into an overall chronology or by highlighting concepts such as 'change' and 'difference' to assist children to see how things develop over time. In the final analysis it can be seen that the National Curriculum history programme offers considerable room for individual planning to suit needs, but schools need to consider:

• how far their choice of units provides a balance of perspectives, for example social, political and cultural, and how far it includes the lives of both 'famous' and ordinary people;
• how far their choice is 'economical', in the sense that it allows good links with other subjects, for example, the 'Ships and seafarers' unit could be seen as offering excellent opportunities in science, technology, geography and English;
• how far their resources would allow them to teach certain units and how they need to plan to make new purchases to widen their curriculum;
• how far they are reflecting the cultural and religious backgrounds of their communities and how far there is a need to extend the teaching to ensure that the children do not end up with a narrow view of history.

About this book

This book is designed to act as a simple reference guide for history teaching. It is intended to provide the busy teacher with some simple ideas that can be incorporated into a teaching programme of National Curriculum history. The book does not prescribe any single method of teaching history; that is left to the teacher's professional discretion. However, the many activities in this book could be used:
• to introduce children to a study unit;
• as practical links in a programme of formal lessons;
• to supplement teacher-designed or commercial scheme material;
• as 'one-off' activities for occasional lessons.

CHAPTER 1

Introducing an historical perspective

At Key Stage 1, the central aim in teaching history is to ensure that children understand that there is a 'past' which can be described, measured, talked about and discovered. Although Key Stage 1 is seen as a whole, there clearly needs to be a series of activities which progressively develop an historical perspective. This chapter introduces simple ideas for children in Reception and Year 1 which focus on:

• conventions of time: now, then, days of the week, months, years and so on;
• the children's own histories;
• events in the children's lives and of the adults around them;
• some stories about the past.

It is important to ensure that history is not just a series of unrelated lessons.

The activities suggested here are all intended to provide an historical link to a wider topic or to be used as ideas in an historical topic. The four elements listed above provide a helpful guide to the overall development of historical concepts across Reception and Year 1, but it is also worth bearing in mind the guidelines set out in the Introduction about curriculum planning.

ACTIVITIES

1. A day in the life of...

Age range
Five to six.

Group size
Individuals.

Topic link
Ourselves.

What you need
Photocopiable page 170 cut up into individual pictures.

What to do
The basic chronology for a young child is that associated with her own daily routine. Give each child the pictures from photocopiable page 170 and ask them to identify what is happening in each picture.

Can the children guess the time of day shown in each picture? They may be quite general, talking of 'morning', 'lunch', 'bedtime' or they may be more specific and talk about definite times such as 'a quarter to eight' or 'half-past five', even if they do not understand the meaning of the times. Ask the children what time of the day they like the best and why and then let them try to put the pictures in the correct chronological order. By doing so, the children will each have created their first time-line.

Further activities
Ask the children to draw pictures of their own and add them to their time-lines.

You might like to make your own time-line showing the four seasons, using one picture for each season. The children could then gather together other pictures or artefacts associated with each season and create a time-line display of the seasons around the room.

2. Me!

Age range
Five to six.

Group size
Individuals.

Topic links
Ourselves, Growing up and Babies.

What you need
Photographs, brought in by the children, which show different stages of their lives.

What to do
Children love opportunities to bring in photographs of themselves, particularly ones that show them as very young children or babies. The children could use photocopies of the photographs, if they are particularly precious, or the photographs could be put in plastic wallets to protect them if they are to be handled by other children.

Ask the children to each arrange the photographs of

themselves in order of age, so that the one showing them at their youngest is first. If the children are able to, they could also write a sentence or two about each photograph. Ask them to say what age they are now and what age they think they were when the photographs were taken. This allows you to introduce the idea of years; for example, 'This happened in 1989 when you were two years old.' Although the children might not understand the passage of time, they will begin to learn about 'the past' and how things happened in different years in the past.

The children could then go on to place themselves in a longer time-line. You could ask their parents to send in details of the names and dates of birth of other children and adults in the family. They will then be able to see how the year in which they were born relates to other members of their family. If the children are able to bring in photographs of other members of their families so much the better.

Finally, the children can make a large time-line in the form of a wall picture; for example, a train with a number of carriages, one for each member of the family, the engine being for the parents and other adults.

Further activity

Ask the children to tell stories to the rest of the class about how they felt before they came to school, and what they remember about being a baby.

3. Reasons

Age range
Five to six.

Group size
The whole class or small groups.

Topic link
No direct topic link.

What you need
No special requirements.

What to do
As history work develops, the children will begin to see that people do things for reasons. They can be helped to understand this if they begin to give reasons for their own actions and speculate on the reasons behind the actions of other people. In small groups or with the whole class describe a number of actions and ask the children to discuss what reasons they think lie behind the actions. Actions could include such things as:
• the head teacher not being happy with the children during the school assembly;
• the Council painting yellow zigzag lines outside the school gates;
• reorganising the classroom

so that the children do not sit next to their friends.

The children could then start to think about good reasons and bad reasons for particular actions and they might also consider actions which appear to take place for no apparent reasons!

Invite one of the children to describe something that he has done and ask his friends to think about the reasons behind his action. They can then ask the child concerned to describe his own reasons for what he did.

Further activities
Ask the children to make a wall display based on one of the decisions described previously. They can use speech bubbles giving the 'good' and 'bad' reasons for what was done on each side or they could make a set of cards that show a number of different reasons on them, for example, 'He felt like doing it', 'It was the safe thing to do', 'She had asked her Mum first' and so on. Then suggest an action to the children. They should respond by choosing from the different reason cards, placing them in two groups, one for good and one for bad reasons.

4. Tell me a tale

Age range
Five to six.

Group size
The whole class or small groups.

Topic link
Fantastic creatures.

What you need
A collection of stories or extracts from stories about the past, some true such as the Gunpowder Plot, the Great Fire of London, Grace Darling and so on, and some myths or fairytales such as Greek myths like Theseus and the Minotaur, the story of Persephone or tales such as St George and the dragon.

What to do
Children can be introduced to the past through stories. This allows them to learn to distinguish between true and fictional stories.

Once you have told the children a story you will need to ask them questions like the following ones.
• Did this really happen and why do you think this happened?
• Why was this story told if it did not happen?
• What does the story tell us about the time in which it was set?

Further activities
Ask the children to list all the mythical creatures and people they have read about or heard about. These could include leprechauns, dragons, unicorns, the phoenix, mermaids, sea serpents and such like. The children could also paint or draw what they think these creatures look like. Better still, they could make a life-size model of one of the creatures and include it in a display of other mythical creatures from the past and from stories and books.

5. Mum at my age

Age range
Five to six.

Group size
Individuals or small groups.

Topic link
Families.

What you need
Photographs of the children's parents, or carers, when they were very young, artefacts such as toys and clothes from the same period.

What to do
Children are often fascinated by the thought of their parents being young children. Begin by asking the children what they think their parents might have been like at the age of five or six. Initially, they are likely to focus on personal characteristics such as height and weight, but encourage them to think further by asking them questions.
• What sort of clothes do you think they wore?
• What games would they have played?

- Where did they live?
- Did they have any brothers and sisters?

Ideally, the way to develop this idea is to ask the parents to co-operate by coming into school and bringing with them photographs and other artefacts of the time. You could also help to supplement this by estimating the range of years in which the parents would have been starting school and try to bring in books, pictures and other artefacts from these years.

Further activity
Repeat this activity but with grandparents – the contrasts are likely to be even starker!

6. Old photographs

Age range
Five to six.

Group size
Groups of three or four.

Topic links
Clothes, Transport, Houses and homes – depending on the content of the photographs.

What you need
A set of old photographs and illustrations on a variety of subjects such as domestic life, transport, clothes, shops and so on.

What to do
Children need to begin to use historical 'evidence' to form opinions and make judgements about the past. Essentially there are two things that can be done with old photographs and illustrations. First, they can be used as a basis for studying the evidence itself. Some children will assume that old photographs are the same as illustrations. Therefore, it is worth letting them look at a photograph taken, for example, 50 years ago and an illustration of something from 50 years ago. What do they notice about the conditions and colour of the photograph as opposed to the illustration?

Second, the children can use the photographs and illustrations to look for similarities and differences between the past and the present. For example, looking at pictures of clothes from the 1920s and comparing them with pictures of clothes from the 1990s. Do shoes look similar? Are there differences in the clothes worn by children? Do the clothes of the 1990s have more patterns on them?

Further activity
A similar exercise can be undertaken with old newspapers. It might be possible to have an actual copy of an old newspaper and a facsimile copy. Can the children tell the difference?

7. It happened last year: 1

Age range
Five to six.

Group size
The whole class.

Topic link
People who help us.

What you need
Two adults who were present at or witnessed the same event.

What to do
Interpretations of the past vary, even when events or actions have been witnessed by the same people. Choose an event that two adults were at in the relatively recent past (no more than six months ago). It would add another dimension if it was also something the children had been present at like a Christmas show, sports day or a class assembly.

Begin by asking the adults to tell the children what they remember about the day and what the highlights were for them. Then ask the children if they can tell you how the accounts were similar or different. Why might one adult remember one aspect of the Christmas show and not another? Did it depend on what role they were playing and where they were situated?

If the children were present at the same event ask them for their memories; for example, it could be that one child's overriding memory of the school sports day is of falling down and hurting herself. You could then ask the children to consider why some people's memories are affected by particular happenings.

Further activity
Invite a local police officer in to the classroom to talk about how the police piece together all the different accounts of an incident. What happens when two witnesses give very different accounts of the same event?

8. It happened last year: 2

Age range
Five to six.

Group size
The whole class and small groups.

Topic link
People who help us.

What you need
A range of items such as photographs, programmes and tickets that are associated with an event that took place in school in the recent past.

What to do
In the previous activity witnesses were asked to recount what they could remember about an event in the recent past. Extend this by gathering a wider range of evidence about the same event. Clearly, this needs to be an event for which 'records' would have survived. So, for example, 'The School at Christmas' might be a good theme because photographs would have been taken, programmes and tickets published for special events, costumes made for plays and so on.

In addition, the children themselves might be able to bring in items associated with the event. More formal records will also exist – you could ask the head teacher to tell the children how the school log book described the event (school registers would also show who was present, dinner registers would show who ate what and so on). Visitors to the school could also be approached and asked to describe what they remember.

You could also extend this activity by looking at what was happening in the wider world at the same time. It might be possible to get a back copy of a newspaper or a comic published at the same time as the special event.

Further activities
Use all the artefacts that have been collected to create an exhibition. You can present tickets and programmes, appoint guides and invite visitors to attend. Such an exhibition is best done when a national event is being commemorated and special events and exhibitions are being held countrywide.

9. A class museum

Age range
Five to six.

Group size
The whole class.

Topic link
No direct topic link.

What you need
A range of artefacts brought in by the children.

What to do
Young children love to bring things into school. For a week or so, ask the children to bring in items from the past and set up a class museum. Clearly, the children will want to talk about what they bring in and time should be set aside for this each day. The children can be asked to talk about:
• what the item is;
• who it belongs to;
• where it came from;
• what use, if any, is made of it now.

When a number of items have been brought in, ask the children how they want their museum arranged. Do they want all similar items such as clothes and newspapers grouped together or would they rather have items from a certain period put together? They may well wish that the items are grouped together to create an attractive display.

Ask the children to think about where in the classroom the museum should be located. They could draw upon any previous experiences of seeing pictures and other items fade if they are exposed to direct sunlight for too long.

Finally, the children should think about labelling the items. This need not be done in writing as, provided all the items are numbered, a description of each item could be recorded on to a cassette tape. Children and visitors to the classroom could then be encouraged to listen to the tape.

Further activity
Arrange a visit to a local museum and look at how the items are displayed. Have they been displayed in a similar way to the items in the class museum?

10. People who help us

Age range
Five to six.

Group size
The whole class and small groups.

Topic link
People who help us.

What you need
Visitors, artefacts, photographs and so on that relate to the history of public services.

What to do
'People who help us' is always a popular topic with young children and it can act as a useful historical study as well. Materials relating to the history of public services are usually available for viewing or loan. Uniforms are a good example of such materials. The children could look at uniforms, for example, of the police and see how these have changed over time. They could also look at transport such as old ambulances and fire engines.

Such a topic also allows for the development of time-lines made up from photographs and artefacts. Oral evidence is also important. You could invite a retired nurse or doctor to talk about how things used to be in the past or ask other people, such as grandparents, to describe what they remember about public services when they were young.

Further activity
The children could also be told stories about people such as Sir Robert Peel and Florence Nightingale (see also activity 4 on page 18).

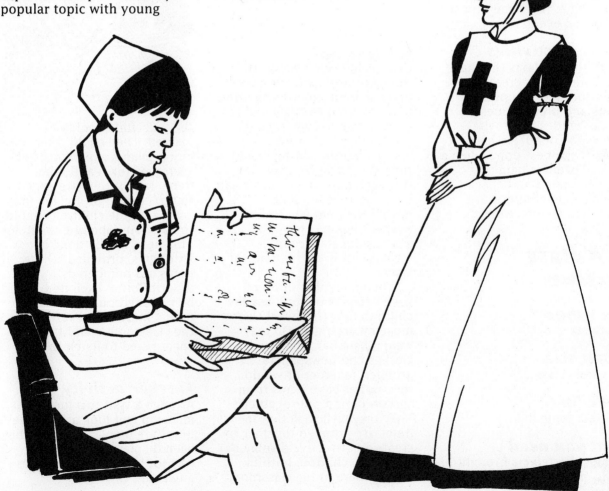

CHAPTER 2

Developing an historical perspective

This chapter contains ideas for children in Year 2. At this stage, the focus will be on:
• local studies which develop a sense of chronology;

• stories which build on earlier work and help children to distinguish between fantasy and reality;
• festivals, ceremonies and

anniversaries which help give an understanding of local, national and world history;
• the use of artefacts and pictures to study the past.

ACTIVITIES

1. Old and new

Age range
Six to seven.

Group size
Groups of three to four.

Topic link
No direct topic link.

What you need
A range of artefacts of various ages – these could include clothes, newspapers, money, household objects such as irons and vacuum cleaners, old toys and so on.

What to do
Children can develop a sense of chronology and understanding of the past by being able to handle historical artefacts. Ideally, you would have one type of artefact, from different periods of history, available for examination; although this is unlikely unless you have access to a private collection or museum. However, a range of artefacts will prove to be equally sufficient for the purpose of this activity.

Ask the children to begin by classifying the objects according to their own criteria; for example, 'This is really old' or 'This is not very old at all'. If they are thinking on the right lines ask them to be more specific and arrange the objects in order of age. How do they assess the age of an item? Are they looking at outward signs of age such as rust, yellowing paper and worn out material, or (and) are they looking for actual 'hard' evidence such as issue dates on newspapers or dates of manufacture on objects? Ask the children to write up the results of their work, identifying what the major factors were in helping them to reach a decision about the age of an item.

If there are no real clues as to the age of an object, you might need to prompt the children to look at reference books. However, make sure that they choose for themselves the appropriate reference book if it is subject specific. If the book is era or date specific, you could encourage the children to use the contents page or index to find information about their artefact.

2. Talking to grandparents

Age range
Six to seven.

Group size
Individuals, small groups or the whole class.

Topic link
Families.

What you need
An elderly person (or people), tape recorder.

What to do
Children need to realise that people are the prime source of information about the past. This can best be demonstrated by inviting a grandparent into the school and asking him to describe what life was like when he was a child. To make best use of this event, it is important to do some background preparation with the children before the visit. Find out the approximate age of the visitor so that you have some idea of the period in history when he was a child. Ask the visitor, in advance, if he can remember any special national or international events. If you or your visitor can bring in artefacts from the period or show pictures, so much the better. This way the children will begin to form a mental picture of the period to which the visitor is referring.

Discuss with the children the sorts of questions they might ask. Themes could include:
• school life;
• games that were played;
• home life;
• food;
• transport;
• entertainment.

Ask each child to prepare a question in advance. If you can acquire some additional biographical information about your visitor, a group of children could prepare a little presentation with which to introduce him. When the visitor comes, tape the discussion.

Further activities
If the visitor is able to bring in photographs or other mementoes, these could be used to prepare a book about his life.

Ask the children to draw pictures, play games of the period, learn songs and dress up as their visitor would have done when he was a child. If the visitor had remembered a special event such as Queen Elizabeth II's coronation, the children could dramatise this and present it.

Finally, set up a tea party and invite your visitor back to the classroom. The children can then present what they have learned about the times when their visitor was a child.

3. Differences

Age range
Six to seven.

Group size
The whole class.

Topic links
Houses and homes, Churches and Shops.

What you need
Pictures of different buildings such as churches, houses and shops from different periods in history.

What to do
Talking about the differences between buildings from different periods in history will help to give the children an understanding of continuity and change. Churches are a good type of building to study. The children should begin by looking for features that are common to the type of building through the ages. With churches, for example, it is likely that a cross will always be present in some shape or form within the building. The same is true of an altar. However, there will also be differences, for example the materials the church is made from or the size of the building.

This work could be extended by taking the children to visit churches in the locality, particularly if there are several from different periods.

From looking at the exterior of the buildings, the children could then look at different patterns of use. For example, what sort of things might a Victorian corner shop have sold? Would this be the same as a corner shop today? They could then go on to explain such differences and, in the case of shops, they might look at supermarkets and think of how they have changed patterns of shopping over time.

Further activities
Ask the children to create models of buildings from different periods in history. They could also compile lists from the evidence they had collected on particular buildings of all the things that are the same and all the things that are different now compared with the past.

4. A family tree

Age range
Six to seven.

Group size
Individuals.

Topic link
Families.

What you need
Photographs of the members of each child's family or photographs of a 'fictitious' family.

What to do
Family relationships provide a good starting point for younger children's understanding of history. However, this issue has to be handled with sensitivity.

Photographs can generate emotions or highlight differences, for example between those children who are looked after by two parents and those who are looked after by one parent. Ask the children to bring in photographs of members of their families. The children should talk about them and describe the different relationships between the members such as 'brother', 'sister', 'mum', 'dad' and so on. Additionally, encourage them to use vocabulary such as 'older' and 'younger'. The children can then begin to create a very simple family tree. The structure should look something like the illustration shown below.

Ideally, the children should stick a photograph of each person beside his or her name or they could draw a picture of each person. Additionally, if the children know the dates of birth of their family members, these could be put in beside each name too. To show how a family tree is built up over time, you could put up your own family tree showing your parents, grandparents and children.

Further activity
See how far back the children can go in tracing their families, for example, they may be able to bring in family mementos which date back over a number of generations. Have they heard any good stories about members of their own families, either present or past? Each child could build up her own family album, finding out as much as she can about her family, including houses that they have lived in, places they have visited on holiday, family members who have moved away and so on.

5. Cars, cars, cars

Age range
Six to seven.

Group size
Individuals.

Topic links
Cars, Transport.

What you need
Photocopiable page 171.

What to do
Cars are very familiar to young children, but how much do they know about cars in the past? Before providing them with photocopiable page 171, ask them what they know about cars in the past. They may have seen films or read books about old cars and will be able to draw upon this knowledge. However, it is unlikely that they will be able to date the cars from the past that they know about.

Provide the children with photocopiable page 171 and ask them to compare the car from the 1900s with the one from the 1940s. What are the main differences which they can see between them? Can they find any other clues about the 1900s from the picture?

Next the children can compare the car from the

Brian (me) aged 6

(Alan Green) Dad

Mum (Muriel Smith)

Colin (my brother) aged 3

Claire (my sister) aged 2

1940s with the car from the 1960s. Where the space has been left on the sheet for the car from the present day, the children could either cut out a photograph and stick it in or draw a picture. They will then be able to compare the car from the 1900s with the car from today.

Finally, don't forget to make available reference books on cars and transport so that the children can see the development of a variety of cars over time.

Further activity
The children could ask their parents to describe different cars they have owned. What do they remember about the cars? What did they like or dislike about each car? Do they have any 'evidence' about their cars such as photographs, number plates, log books and so on.

6. Facts and opinions

Age range
Six to seven.

Group size
Individuals or small groups.

Topic link
No direct topic link.

What you need
A number of written statements of fact (for example, 'The Second World War began in 1939') and statements of opinion (for example, 'The Second World War should not have taken place') about historical events.

What to do
The children will have been introduced to the past through stories about famous events and people. This will have given them an awareness of certain things about the past. However, they need to begin to appreciate the difference between facts about the past

and opinions about the past. This will need to be put into language that the children will understand and so the distinction between the two can be described as:
• what we *know* about things that happened in the past;
• what people *think* about things that happened in the past.

In the first category, the children can be introduced to the concept of 'evidence', or how we know what we know about the past. So, begin by recounting a famous event or story from the past, for example, the story of Florence Nightingale, the story of King Alfred or of the coronation of Queen Elizabeth II. Then provide some statements about the event or story making sure that you have two categories of statement; for example, statements in the first category might be:
• Florence Nightingale assisted wounded soldiers during the Crimean War.
• King Alfred was a king of Wessex.
• Huge crowds turned out to see the coronation of Queen Elizabeth II.

Examples of statements in the second category might be:
• Many people were killed during the Crimean War who shouldn't have been.

• King Alfred was a wicked king.
• The Queen should rule over the country.

The children will naturally be inclined to treat statements from the second category as statements of fact. This is where the emphasis on evidence becomes important.

Further activity
Encourage the children to make judgements about the facts they hear about the past.

7. The saints

Age range
Six to seven.

Group size
Individuals, small groups or the whole class.

Topic links
Customs and festivals, Countries of the United Kingdom.

What you need
Story-books and reference books about the lives of the saints.

What to do
Begin by asking the children if they know about any of the saints – they might even be in a school which is named after a saint. Depending on the children's religious background, they might already know quite a bit about the saints. Ask them to think about the evidence they have about the lives of the saints. They might have stories from the Bible or they might have reports written by contemporaries about the lives of certain saints. The children should decide how much they know with certainty and how much they are less certain about. Clearly, this has to be handled with sensitivity in recognition of children's cultural and religious backgrounds.

The children could go on to look at the patron saints of the British Isles.
• What is known about each of them?
• Which day is each one's special feast day?

• What symbols or stories are associated with them (for example, St George and the dragon and St Andrew and the cross)?

The children could then act out particular episodes from the lives of the saints and prepare a presentation or assembly for other classes in the school. This could also be linked with a topic on the customs and festivals of countries in the United Kingdom.

Further activity
Encourage the children to use reference books to find out further background information about other saints. Could they make up their own book entitled 'The Lives of Saints' with stories and pictures about a number of saints?

8. Christmas

Age range
Six to seven.

Group size
Individuals or small groups.

Topic links
Christmas.

What you need
Reference books about Christmas.

What to do
Although Christmas is an extremely busy time in the school year, it does offer opportunities for historical study. Essentially, it is a festival celebrating something that happened in the past. Ask the children to think about the Christmas story and where evidence for it comes from. Ask them to make a list of all the traditions associated with Christmas and see how much they can find out about their origins using the reference books. They could research about:
• Father Christmas;
• giving and receiving presents;
• Christmas trees;
• Christmas puddings;
• Christmas carols.

You could also introduce the children to how Christmas was celebrated in the past, for example, a Victorian Christmas. What was done that is the same as at Christmas today? What is different from Christmas today? What can be found out from stories about Victorian Christmases and what can be found out from sources such as newspapers and letters?

Further activity
Use other festivals and celebrations to encourage the children to look at the origins of such events. These could include:
• Easter;
• Harvest;
• Bonfire Night;
• Pancake Day;
• Mothers Day;
• Diwali;
• Hannukah.

CHAPTER 3

Invaders and settlers: Romans, Anglo-Saxons and Vikings in Britain

The intention of this chapter is to introduce children to the early history of the British Isles. In particular, it is important to show how British society was shaped and changed by a succession of invading peoples with different cultures, languages and influences.

This unit of the National Curriculum covers a long span of time and therefore it is best taught in chronological sequence. However, the National Curriculum specifies that children should be given the opportunity to study in greater depth one of the three invasions. This study would include an examination of what prompted the invasion, what the invaders found when they arrived in Britain and how they changed aspects of society over time.

BACKGROUND

The Romans

Although Julius Caesar invaded Britain in 55 and 54BC, it was not until AD43 that major Roman settlements appeared in Britain, when the Emperor Claudius conquered eastern and southern Britain. He called his son Britannicus in honour of his victory. The commander of the army, Aulus Plautius, became the first Roman governor of the province.

Over time, the Romans extended their control and by AD51, the second governor, Ostorius Scapula, had defeated the British king, Caratacus, in Wales. Ten years later, Boudicca, Queen of the Iceni in eastern Britain, was killed having led resistance against the Romans. In AD78, Julius Agricola was made governor of Britain. Much then becomes known about this period because the writer, Tacitus, was married to Agricola's daughter and Tacitus described in detail the Romanisation of Britain

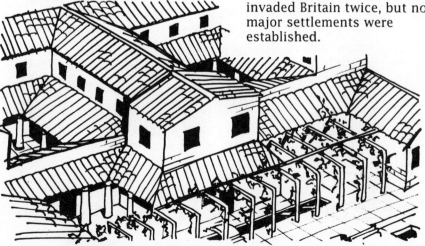

including the laying of roads and the introduction of under-floor heating systems.

The next major development came under the Emperor Hadrian. In AD122 he came to Britain, having spent a number of years travelling around his empire ensuring that it was safe from invaders. He was particularly concerned that even though Agricola had won battles in Scotland, the defences against the Scots had been weakened as Agricola's soldiers were required elsewhere in the Empire. Hadrian, therefore, decided to build a wall to keep the Scots at bay.

Many elements of Roman civilisation were brought to Britain. For example, the British had previously lived in small wooden houses on hill tops. The Romans demonstrated that it was better to build homes of stone on lower ground.

Key dates

• 55 and 54BC: Julius Caeser invaded Britain twice, but no major settlements were established.

• AD43: Claudius invaded Britain, adding the southern part of the country to his empire.
• AD51: British king, Caratacus, defeated by Ostorius Scapula.
• AD78: Julius Agricola made governor of Britain.
• AD122–126: Hadrian's Wall built in northern Britain.

Teaching plan

A series of lessons and activities on the Romans could be structured as follows.
• The background and history of the Roman empire.
• Expansion and invasion: the motivation behind invasion and key events and characters.
• Resistance to Roman rule.
• The Roman army in Britain.
• The structure of Roman society: citizens, subjects and slaves.
• Family life and home life in Roman Britain.
• Roman housing and architecture.
• Worship and sacrifice.
• The departure of the Romans.

There are also many parts of Britain where Roman remains are still in evidence, for example Bath, York, Colchester and Northumberland. If it is at all possible, you should try to include visits to Roman sites.

The activities which follow could be included as part of the teaching plan described above. Although this unit could be taught at any year during Key Stage 2, an indication has been given of the most suitable age range for each activity.

ACTIVITIES

1. The Roman gods

Age range
Seven to eleven.

Group size
Individuals or small groups.

What you need
A list of the Roman gods (see below), old blankets and sheets to make Roman costumes.

What to do
The Romans believed in many gods and goddesses and brought such beliefs with them to Britain. They believed that if they pleased the gods, then the gods would bring them good luck. Many stories were told about the gods and these were used to teach moral lessons or describe what would happen if the gods were displeased.

The Roman gods, included gods to protect the house, gods of healing, gods of farming and so on. The two most important gods were:
• Jupiter – god of the sky and king of all the gods;
• Juno – wife of Jupiter, goddess of women and mothers.

The Romans believed that the other gods were related to Jupiter and Juno. Some of the most important ones were:
• Bacchus – god of wine;
• Diana – goddess of the moon and hunting;
• Janus – god of doorways and journeys;
• Mars – god of war;
• Mercury – messenger of the gods and the god of trade;
• Venus – goddess of love and beauty;
• Vulcan • god of fire.

Ask the children to devise a story using one of the gods listed above. Remind them that the purpose of their story is to make a point or reinforce a moral. For example, a story about Mars could be about him fighting his enemies and defeating them for ever. This story should then emphasise the point that Mars should be worshipped before every battle to ensure victory.

When the children have written their stories, they could dramatise them. However, they would have to adapt their stories so that gods were not portrayed as the Romans considered it sacrilegious for gods to be portrayed by mortals.

Tell the children to find out about Roman theatre. They will probably find that the Romans generally preferred comedies to tragedies and that they also enjoyed mime, when a story was accompanied by music or singing. Masks too played an important part in Roman drama and the children could devise their own masks appropriate to the themes of their stories. They will also discover that women could only appear in mimes. Why do children think this was so, considering that some of the gods were female?

Further activities
Ask the children to find the equivalent Greek names of the Roman gods. They could also investigate why the Christians refused to worship the Roman gods and what happened to the Christians as a result.

2. A Roman soldier on Hadrian's Wall

Age range
Seven to eleven.

Group size
Individuals.

What you need
A map of Britain detailing Hadrian's Wall (ancient or modern), reference books which show Roman soldiers (their uniforms, weapons and so on) paper, cold tea, writing implement, ink.

What to do
The Roman Empire depended on a strong and efficient army to defend its frontiers and Hadrian's wall was at the northern fringes of the Empire. Ask the children to imagine that they are Roman legionnaires serving on Hadrian's Wall and write a letter back to their families in Rome describing what life is like for them. In order for the children to undertake this task with any degree of empathy, they need to understand something of the physical conditions in Northumbria at the time. Use the map to discover something about the terrain of the area and describe to the children, the kind of equipment which the legionary would have carried including helmet, metal jacket, tunic, belt, weapons such as swords, javelins and daggers and walking shoes. The children should describe what they think it was like to live in a Roman fort, how the legionaries would spend their day and what happened when the barbarians attacked. (Generally, the Wall was patrolled by auxiliary soldiers with the elite legionary troops being called in when there was serious trouble).

The children could then make their own Roman paper to write on by screwing up pieces of paper and soaking them in cold tea. The paper can then be flattened out, dried and written on using ink.

Further activity
Using a map showing Roman settlement in Britain, the children could mark on to a present day map where Roman walls and forts were situated. They can then consider why legionaries would find some assignments better than others.

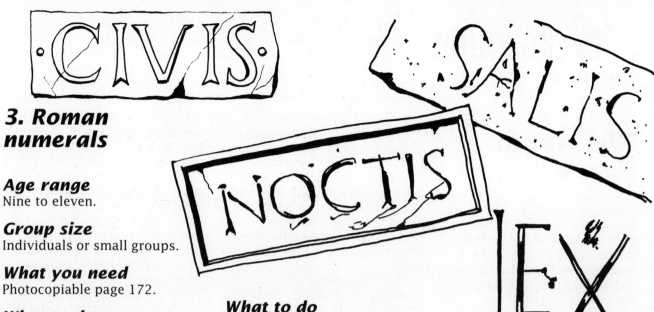

3. Roman numerals

Age range
Nine to eleven.

Group size
Individuals or small groups.

What you need
Photocopiable page 172.

What to do
Unlike the Arabic numbers we use today, Roman numerals were written as strings of letters. Photocopiable page 172 shows the most common Roman numerals and indicates how larger numbers were constructed by adding on different letters. Let the children use this sheet to make up their own numbers such as the years they, or other members of their family, were born.

Further activities
Ask the children to find where Roman numerals are still in use. Why do they think that such numbers are used at the end of television programmes or films?

4. Latin links

Age range
Ten to eleven.

Group size
Individuals or small groups.

What you need
Dictionaries.

What to do
Latin was spoken by those in government in all the lands the Romans ruled. Most of the conquered peoples would have continued to speak their own languages on a day to day basis. Latin was the language of international communication, government and trade. Even today, Latin remains the basis of many other languages including English. Give the children the Latin words listed below but don't tell them what they mean – instead see if they can work them out for themselves!
Latin:
aqua (*aquae*)
lex (*legis*)
civis (*civis*)
communis (*communis*)
populus (*populi*)
nox (*noctis*)
sal (*salis*)
turris (*turris*)

English meaning:
water
law
citizen
common
people
night
salt
tower

The word in brackets beside each Latin word is the genitive, or possessive form. It is this that often forms the basis of words in English.
What other words can the children find from each of these Latin roots? They should use a dictionary to help them.

Further activities
Can the children find other words which have come from Latin? If you have access to dictionaries from English to other modern European languages, it might be possible to see whether words, from other languages which have Latin origins look similar to their English form. Can the children find examples of where Latin is still used or seen, for example, in a school motto? Ask them why they think that Latin is used in such cases. There is no simple answer as to why Latin was so popular. However, the associations with learning and the church may be an important factor.

BACKGROUND

The Anglo Saxons

From the year AD230 onwards, Saxon pirates began to raid the east coast of Britain for slaves, cattle and valuable jewellery. At first, the Romans resisted these attacks and responded by sending additional troops to Britain from other parts of the Empire and establishing better defences. However, by AD360, Britain was under attack from all sides. The Picts were raiding the northern borders, the Scots, based in Ireland, were attacking the west coast and Saxons from Germany were continuing their attacks from the east. By AD410, the Emperor Honorius had told the Britons that he was

withdrawing all the Roman soldiers as they were needed to defend Rome itself from barbarians. Immediately after the Romans left there was no large-scale invasion. Rather, over time, the invaders realised that they would meet little resistance if they came to settle.

These invaders, who replaced the Romans, came mainly from Holland, North Germany and Denmark. Collectively they came to be known as the Anglo-Saxons or the Saxons, but were made up of many Germanic peoples including Angles, Jutes and Frisians.

In about AD450, the Saxons, led by Hengest and Horsa, fought against Vortigern who

was the king of much of Britain and, as a consequence, expanded their power over much of southern England. When the warriors had seized a patch of country, they established a *Bretwalda* meaning 'Britain-ruler'. This ruler became more powerful by increasing the land that he ruled over.

Many legends have grown up about King Arthur. Little is known about him except that it is likely that he was a leader of the Britons, in the sixth century, who resisted the Anglo-Saxons on a number of occasions.

By AD600 or 700, a number of small kingdoms had emerged. At any one time, there were likely to be seven powerful kingdoms in the land, the so-called Heptarchy. However, it was not until AD757 that one king, Offa, regarded himself as ruler of all England.

During the fifth and sixth centuries, the Celtic church grew from strength to strength in areas of Britain that had not been overrun by the English invaders. This conversion was achieved by the Irish saints, Patrick, Columba and Aidan. In AD597, Augustine arrived in Britain from Rome. He had been sent by Pope Gregory I to bring Christianity to England. However, there were areas of conflict between the Roman and Celtic missions and it was not until AD663 that the whole of the British church was united to Rome after the Synod of Whitby.

Key dates

AD230: Saxon pirates began their attacks on the east coast of Britain.
AD376: Major defeat for the Roman Army inflicted by the combined efforts of the Saxons, Picts and Scots.
AD410: Roman armies withdrew from Britain.
AD450: Defeat of Vortigern by the Saxon brothers, Hengest and Horsa.
AD400–600: The so-called 'Dark Ages', about which little about the history of Britain is known.
AD597: St Augustine began his mission to Britain.
AD663: Synod of Whitby.
AD757–796: King Offa regards himself as ruler of all England.

Teaching plan

A series of lessons and activities on the Anglo-Saxons could be structured as follows.
• The end of Roman rule in Britain and the invasions of the Saxons.
• Who were the Angles and Saxons and where did they come from?
• Anglo-Saxon kingdoms, homes and domestic life.
• The legend of King Arthur.
• The Dark Ages.
• The Seven Kingdoms.
• The coming of Christianity to Britain.

ACTIVITIES

1. The departure of the Romans

Age range
Seven to eleven.

Group size
Maximum of three or four.

What you need
Extracts from the writings of the period such as *De Excido et Conquestu Britanniae* (ascribed to Gildas and thought to have been written shortly before AD548), reference books about Anglo-Saxons.

What to do
As the Roman forces in Britain became more depleted, it became clear to the Britons that the new invaders were likely to bring many changes. One contemporary historian, Gildas, described the Picts and Scots as 'foul hosts' with a 'lust for blood' and 'hang-dog faces'. He described how they pulled the Britons down from Hadrian's Wall and slaughtered them as 'lambs by butchers'.

In a letter to Rome, Gildas wrote, 'The barbarians drive us to the sea; the sea drives us to the barbarians; between these two methods of death, we are either massacred or drowned.'

Let the children study these accounts and then ask them to write a reply to Gildas' letter as if they were a friend offering advice. They could also draw pictures of the invaders, using the powerful descriptions, provided by Gildas, to help them.

Ask the children to find out as much as they can about the Anglo-Saxons using reference books. Can they find out the answers to some of the following questions?
• Where did the Anglo-Saxons come from?
• Why did they invade?
• How did they reach Britain?

Further activity
Could the children design and make their own Anglo-Saxon longboat? From remains of such a boat found in Denmark, these boats are thought to have been narrow-beamed, low-sided, made of overlapping planks (dinker-build) and without a mast or sail. Such boats were powered by fourteen pairs of oarsmen and were capable of holding thirty or forty warriors.

2. An Anglo-Saxon poem

Age range
Eight to eleven.

Group size
The whole class.

What you need
A copy of the epic poem *Beowulf* (extracts from this and other Anglo-Saxon poetry can be found in *Anglo-Saxon Poetry*, edited by R.K. Gordon [1954] Dent Everyman).

What to do

The poem *Beowulf* was written by an unknown Northumbrian monk. It was a traditional story which minstrels had been singing for hundreds of years before the poem was written. It describes heroes and monsters and uses highly descriptive language.

Take two or three extracts from the poem and read them to the children. What do they notice about the language and the imagery? Tell the children that, as a whole class, you are going to write your own epic poem using a theme from the Anglo-Saxon times. It could be about St Augustine being sent from Rome to convert the English to Christianity or it could be about one of the great kingdoms of the time. Having decided on the initial story-line, ask the children to supply as many adjectives as they can and then put them in an appropriate order to be written on the board. Then ask the children to read out the list. They could then illustrate their story or dramatise it, imagining that they are a band of travelling minstrels, performing to a village full of people.

Further activity

Ask the children to find out what they can about other writings of the period such as the *Anglo-Saxon Chronicles* or Bede's *Ecclesiastical History*. Ask the children why they think it was mostly monks who carried out all the writing.

3. The Anglo-Saxon kingdoms

Age range
Nine to eleven.

Group size
Individuals.

What you need
Photocopiable page 173, reference books and atlases.

What to do
As the Anglo-Saxons became more established in Britain, so kingdoms emerged around the *Bretwalda* or local overlord. Using photocopiable page 173, the children can see some of the minor and major kingdoms that emerged. Can they find any of the Anglo-Saxon place names on a modern map? Ask the children to use the reference material to find out why each of the places mentioned have significance in the history of the Anglo-Saxons. In particular, they could find out about:
• Iona;
• Jarrow;
• Whitby;
• Sutton Hoo;
• the religious use of Stonehenge;
• Glastonbury.

Further activities
The discovery made at Sutton Hoo in 1939 gave historians and archaeologists their best insight into Saxon Britain. Ask the children to find out about the discoveries at Sutton Hoo. How much do they tell the children about the life of a Saxon king? What questions are left unanswered? Using pictures of the jewellery found at Sutton Hoo, the children could design their own pieces of jewellery. Develop this further and let the children look at illuminated manuscripts from later periods. Perhaps the children could imagine that they are writing a diary entry for the *Anglo-Saxon Chronicle*.

The Vikings

In AD793, the Vikings first attacked Britain, killing and robbing their way through St Cuthbert's monastery on Lindisfarne.

The Vikings were Scandinavian farmers from northern Europe. It is not known exactly why the Vikings took to exploring Europe, but throughout the summer months they attacked virtually every coast of Europe. Over time, the Vikings seized islands in the Orkneys and the Hebrides and used these as starting points for raids to other parts of Britain and Ireland. They organised armies of conquest and bit by bit they conquered large parts of Britain including the area around York, the Midlands and East Anglia.

By AD871 only King Alfred stood against the Vikings, or 'Danes' as they were known. Eventually, after the Battle of Ethandune (or Edington), King Alfred agreed the Peace of Wedmore in AD878 which converted the Danes to Christianity and divided up the kingdom with the Danes ruling England north of Watling Street and Alfred remaining King of Wessex. Alfred had managed to tackle many of the weaknesses that, up until then, had afflicted Saxon Britain. He established a string of fortresses from Wessex to London, he built a fleet of warships to defend the coast, he established laws and courts across the country and he secured a succession of diplomatic alliances both within Britain and with various Viking leaders.

Key dates

AD793: A Viking fleet first attacked Britain (Lindisfarne).
AD836: Viking colony established in Dublin.
AD866: Viking 'Great Army' in England; Northumbria, East Anglia and Mercia overwhelmed. Danish kingdom established at York.
AD871: King Ethelred and Alfred won the Battle of Ashdown and five year truce was established.
AD878: Battle of Ethandune won by Alfred and led to the treaty of Wedmore.
AD899: Death of King Alfred.

Teaching plan

A series of lessons and activities on the Vikings could be structured as follows.
• Who were the Vikings and where did they come from?
• Viking conquests across Europe and beyond.
• Viking longboats.
• Viking trade, farming, fishing and domestic life.
•Viking religion.
• The life and times of King Alfred.

ACTIVITIES

1. Viking gods

Age range
Seven to eleven.

Group size
A maximum of three or four.

What you need
Junk materials such as boxes, card, buttons, foil, paper and so on, references material about Viking gods.

What to do
From what information is available, it would appear that the Viking gods were quite fearsome. The god Odin (Woden) gave gifts such as courage, victory and wisdom, but, in the end, he always did as he chose, paying no heed to prayers or sacrifices. Yet, warriors accepted death because they believed that they would go immediately to Valhalla where there was eternal feasting and battle.

The god Thor was a red-bearded god who was thought to make thunder and lightning. Thunder was caused by him clattering about in the sky, while lightning was caused by him hurling his axe-hammer.

Ask the children to use the junk materials to make large models of Viking gods. They should make them as cruel and pitiless as they can. The children could also write stories about the gods and display them beside their models.

Further activities
The children could find out more about Viking burial rites and religion. In particular they could investigate what happened at the three major festivals of Vetrarblot in mid-October, Jolablot in mid-January and Sigrblot in April.

2. Alfred the Great: factfile

Age range
Eight to eleven.

Group size
Individuals or pairs.

What you need
Reference books about the Anglo-Saxons and Vikings.

What to do
Alfred the Great was the first king of England about whom a reasonable amount is known. Ask the children to create a factfile about him and in particular, let them investigate his relationship with the Danes. Tell the children to find out about the following:
• Who was Alfred's father?
• How did Alfred defeat the Danes at Ethandune?
• What was surprising about how he treated the Danes through the Peace of Wedmore?
• What were the laws he established throughout his kingdom?
• Why was he described by the Victorians as 'Great'?

Further activity
This could be the first of a series of factfiles which the children keep about kings of England. Even though they do not study the next historical period at Key Stage 2, they could begin to read about kings who preceded the Normans such as Edgar the Peaceable and Ethelred the Unready.

3. A Viking house

Age range
Nine to eleven.

Group size
Individuals or pairs.

What you need
Construction wood, lollipop sticks, glue gun, pieces of straw or reed.

What to do
Ask the children to make their own Viking houses using wood. Essentially, Viking houses were built on simple frames and had thatched, reed or straw roofs. There was a raised fireplace in the centre of each house and a small hole in the roof let out the smoke. The house was the centre of Viking activity, but it must have been extremely smelly and dirty because the animals would often also be inside. Can the children capture this in any of their models?

Further activity
The children could imagine that they were Viking children and write about what it was like to live in the house and village, where animals would roam loose around the village and open cess pits were dug at the back of each dwelling. Girls had to be trained to run a household, so they learned to spin, weave and make clothes, ship sails and cargo bags. Boys would sail with the men as soon as they were old enough, but before that, they had to learn how to plough and cut wood. The Vikings enjoyed outdoor games such as winter ice-skating and skiing.

CHAPTER 4

Tudor and Stuart times

This core study unit is designed to introduce children to the key issues, people and events in Tudor and Stuart times. The focus is on people at all levels of society, using the rich amount of documentary evidence available from this period. The children should learn about rulers and court life, people in the towns and in the country, scientific and cultural achievements, exploration and empire and religious issues. In addition to the history of England, the histories of Scotland, Wales and Ireland should also be referred to.

BACKGROUND

The Tudor period began with the accession to the throne of Henry VII in 1485. He was followed by his son who became Henry VIII in 1509. This proved to be the beginning of a turbulent period. Henry fell out with the Pope over the subject of divorce and subsequently became the head of the Church of England. Although Henry was married six times, he only had three surviving heirs. His son, Edward VI, acceded to the throne as a boy and reigned for six years. After his death Henry's daughter, Mary, was crowned. She sought to make England back into a Roman Catholic country. On her death Henry's daughter, Elizabeth, ascended the throne and reigned from 1558 to 1603.

Elizabeth maintained her power even though there were several plots against her, most notably led by Mary, Queen of Scots, who was executed in 1587. A year later, King Philip II of Spain sent his Armada against the English, partly because he resented British attacks against him which were made through the Dutch and also because he resented the way in which people like Drake and Grenville robbed Spanish treasure ships on their way home from the New World. He also felt that, as a devout Catholic, it was his duty to retake England and convert it back to Catholicism. The attack failed however, and Protestantism was firmly established in England.

Elizabeth died in 1603 and was succeeded by King James VI of Scotland who became James I of England. As he was the son of Mary, Queen of Scots, many Catholics believed that he would favour their religion, but this was not to be the case and a number of Catholic nobles began to plot how to kill him. However, the Gunpowder Plot was discovered and the protagonists executed.

The established Protestantism was not to the liking of all Protestants and the Puritans, a group of people who believed in simple worship and a church without elaborate structures, fled to America in 1620 aboard the *Mayflower*.

Matters came to a head with the accession of Charles I in 1625. He believed in the Divine Right of Kings to govern and this led him into direct dispute with Parliament, resulting in civil war between the King and his Cavaliers and Parliament's soldiers, the Roundheads. The Parliamentarians were led by Oliver Cromwell and they finally defeated the Royalists, executing King Charles in 1649. Cromwell became Lord

Protector, refusing to become King. However, when he died, Charles II, the son of Charles I, was restored to the throne.

The reign of Charles II was memorable for a series of disasters. First there was plague in 1665, and this was followed by the Great Fire of London in 1666. Finally, there was the war with Holland which led to the burning of Chatham and Rochester.

James II succeeded Charles, but he was driven from the throne after only three years by his daughter, Mary, and her Dutch husband, William, for seeking to restore Catholicism to the country. The last of the Stuarts was Queen Anne whose reign came to be dominated by others, most notably the Duke of Marlborough.

The Tudor and Stuart times were remarkable for the development of the arts, literature, science and exploration. William Shakespeare, Christopher Marlowe and Ben Johnson were but a few of the writers who were writing during Tudor times, as did men of letters such as Francis Bacon, Walter Raleigh and Richard Markluyt. Stuart times were no less memorable as men like Samuel Pepys, John Milton, John Bunyan and John Donne all flourished.

Key dates

1485: Henry VII came to the throne.
1509: Henry VIII came to the throne.
1534: Act of Supremacy led to Henry exerting control over the English Church.
1547: King Edward VI, the boy king, came to the throne.
1553: Mary became Queen.
1558: Queen Elizabeth I came to the throne.
1587: Execution of Mary, Queen of Scots.
1588: Spanish Armada sailed for England and was defeated.
1603: James VI of Scotland became James I of England. Union of Scottish and English crowns.
1605: Gunpowder Plot.
1611: Authorised Version of the Bible published.
1625: Charles I became King.
1642: Outbreak of English Civil War.
1649: Charles I executed and Cromwell became Lord Protector.

1658: Death of Cromwell.
1660: Restoration of monarchy in Britain under Charles II.
1665: The Plague of London.
1666: The Great Fire of London.
1685: James II of England (James VII of Scotland) became King.
1688: Flight of James II and the 'Glorious Revolution'.
1689: William III and Mary II became King and Queen of England.
1702: Queen Anne became the last Stuart monarch (died 1714).

Teaching plan

A series of lessons and activities on the Tudors and Stuarts could be structured as follows.
• King Henry VII and King Henry VIII and his six wives.
• Mary Queen of Scots.
• The life of Queen Elizabeth I.
• The Spanish Armada.
• William Shakespeare and the Globe Theatre.
• The Gunpowder Plot.
• Samuel Pepys, the Plague and the Great Fire of London.
• Tudor and Stuart homes.
• Domestic life in Tudor and Stuart times.
• Exploration in Tudor and Stuart times.

A topic on the Tudors and Stuarts allows for you to organise special events where the children can dress up in period costume.

ACTIVITIES

1. Tudor guilds

Age range
Seven to eleven.

Group size
Individuals.

What you need
Reference books describing the guilds of craftsmen, thin coloured paper, black card, Blu-Tack.

What to do
All kinds of shops emerged in Tudor times. Shopkeepers would usually belong to a guild which was made up from the craftsmen skilled in a particular area. Apprentices would have to train for a number of years before they were accepted into the guild and thereby allowed to set up their own shops.

Each of the different guilds had its own sign. Ask the children to find out which were the most popular trades of the period and let them design their own guild signs. They can do this on thin coloured paper using black felt-tipped pens to draw thick black lines. These could then be stuck into a black paper frame. Using Blu-Tack the designs can be stuck on to a window so that they resemble the stained-glass windows in a church, where many such signs would have been displayed due to the religious roots of many of the guilds.

Further activity
Ask the children to design guild signs for more recent occupations such as television engineer or firefighter.

2. A banquet for Queen Elizabeth

Age range
Seven to eleven.

Group size
The whole class.

What you need
Tudor costumes for the children, tables laid out for a feast, 'Elizabethan' food such as chicken, bread and raw vegetables; prepared entertainment such as jesters and minstrels.

What to do
Queen Elizabeth and her retinue would often visit various stately homes about the country and during her visit she would be entertained by the local lord of the manor. Organise such a visit for your class. Let the children prepare entertainments for the Queen and lay out the tables and prepare food to eat.

Try to get an adult visitor to dress up as Queen Elizabeth, who can be led into the banqueting hall in a procession.

A foreigner once described Queen Elizabeth as she went to parliament as follows:

'Now followed the queen in a half-covered sedan chair which looked like a half-covered bed. The chair and cushions on which the queen was seated were covered with gold and silver cloth. The queen had a long red velvet parliamentary mantle down to the waist, lined with ermine, white with little black dots and a crown on her head...' (from *Tudors and Stuarts* by R.J. Unstead [1974] A & C Black).

Further activity

Tell the children to write descriptions of their banquet after the event. They should, as far as possible, try to use the forms of language used at the time.

3. The Gunpowder Plot

Age range
Seven to eleven.

Group size
Individuals.

What you need
No special requirements.

What to do
Begin by asking the children what they know about 5 November and Bonfire Night. Ask them if they know anything about its origins. This is an important starting point because it provides an example of a real life historical event which now forms the basis of a modern celebration. It is worthwhile getting the children to write a 'before' and 'after' version of the Gunpowder Plot. The 'before' version would consist of everything that they know about the event before they carry out any research, while the 'after' version would be based on research and study and present the happenings as

an historical event. By the end of the historical study, the children should know more than just 'what happened'. They should know:
• who Guy Fawkes was and where his co-conspirators came from;
• why they were plotting to destroy the Houses of Parliament;
• why they attempted what they did at the beginning of November;
• what happened to them;
• what the origins of Bonfire Night were.

Further activity
Ask the children to think of other special celebrations which are based on historical events or people. How far have these become surrounded by myths?

4. Inside a Tudor home

Age range
Eight to eleven.

Group size
Individuals.

What you need
Photocopiable page 174, reference books about the period.

What to do
Photocopiable page 174 provides an inventory of the furniture in the house of Sir Henry Parker. Although furniture had become more comfortable and elegant, big houses still had comparatively little furniture in them. Ask the children to research the probable style of each of the items described on the sheet and provide a simple illustration.

As a comparison let the children draw up an inventory of all the furniture they have in their houses.
• Why do they think that Tudor houses had so little furniture in them?
• What can they tell about the way the Tudors lived by the furniture in their houses?
• What furniture in houses today is largely dependent on technological advances and new materials becoming available?

Further activity
Try to organise a class visit to an Elizabethan manor house such as Hatfield House, Compton Wynyates or Hampton Court.

5. Plague and fire

Age range
Eight to eleven.

Group size
Individuals.

What you need
Photocopiable page 175.

What to do
Much of what we know about the Plague of 1665 and the Great Fire of London of 1666 comes from the diary of Samuel Pepys. Give each child a copy of photocopiable page 175 which shows several extracts from Pepys's diary. Ask them to imagine that they were writing the diary entries for the next few days. To add an authentic touch they could write their diaries in code, just as Samuel Pepys did. They could then pass over their diary entries and codes to friends to see if they can crack them!

Further activity
Ask the children to consider the reasons why Pepys's diary is an excellent piece of evidence about the Stuart period. However, they should also consider some of its shortcomings, for example, it being the work of only one man and therefore only one view of events which took place.

6. A labourer's lot

Age range
Nine to eleven.

Group size
Individuals.

What you need
No special requirements.

What to do
Working as a landless labourer in Elizabethan times was extremely arduous. Read to the children the following law which was passed early in the sixteenth century and detailed how much time a labourer had to work.

'Every... labourer shall be at work between the middle of the month of March and the middle of the month of September before 5 of the clock in the morning. And that he have but half an hour for his breakfast and an hour and a half for his dinner... And that he depart not from his work between 7 and 8 of the clock in the morning.'
(Taken from *The Tudor Age* by A.F. Scott [*out of print*])

Ask the children to work out how many hours a day or week the landless labourer had to work. They could then compare that with the hours most people have to work today.

Further activity
Let the children research in more detail the respective responsibilities of the different people who owned or worked on the land such as gentry, bailiffs, yeomen and tenants.

7. Understanding Shakespeare

Age range
Nine to eleven.

Group size
Groups of three or four or the whole class.

What you need
Costumes of the Tudor period for the children, extracts from Shakespeare's plays (adapted for easier understanding).

What to do
Primary teachers do not usually tackle Shakespeare as part of a topic on the 'Tudors and Stuarts'. Yet it is important to do so. Shakespeare was a central figure of the age and his Globe Theatre was an important meeting point. Also, his stories are of immense interest to children if they are explained in simple terms. Therefore, for the purpose of this activity, you could either choose actual extracts from one of Shakespeare's plays and let the children dramatise them, for example the witches' speech in *Macbeth* or part of *Julius Caesar*; or, you could describe to the children the story-line and ask them to dramatise the story in their own way using language of the time if possible. The best plays for doing this are probably *King Lear*, *The Tempest* and *Henry V*, each of which has its own memorable scenes.

Further activities
If you lack confidence in Shakespeare, why not contact the English department of your local secondary school and see whether a teacher or some older students would be prepared to run a 'masterclass' for your children? Also, if you have a local theatre company in the area, contact them and see if they would like to visit the school.

In more general terms, as Shakespeare's plays deal with different historical periods, ask the children to consider the influence his work has had in shaping people's perceptions of the past.

8. Portraits of an age

Age range
Nine to eleven.

Group size
Individuals or pairs.

What you need
Copies of portraits in the National Portrait Gallery (available in postcard size) of Henry VIII, Queen Elizabeth I, Sir Francis Drake, Sir Walter Raleigh, William Shakespeare and so on.

What to do
Portraits are extremely valuable pieces of evidence, particularly for the periods before photography. The popular images of historical figures are formed by such portraits and the children can use them to research clothes of the period as well as study physical characteristics. However, the children need to be aware of the limitations of portraits. Ask them to think about:
• when the portrait was painted;
• who the painter was;
• whether the portrait presents a flattering image of the person that is not confirmed by other evidence (for example, there is evidence that the Holbein portrait of Henry VIII was more than flattering to Henry's grosser physique).

Further activity
Introduce the children to ways in which photographs and film are now used to create particular images, for example, in advertising. They could also look at how certain political events are 'stage managed'.

9. The King James Bible

Age range
Nine to eleven.

Group size
Individuals or the whole class.

What you need
Copies of the King James Bible.

What to do
Today only modern versions of the Bible tend to be used in schools and, therefore, children are not as familiar as they once were with the King James version of the Bible. However, when teaching the children about the religious disputes that continued from Queen Elizabeth's reign into the reign of James I, the King James Bible becomes an important text because it came about as a result of the King's desire to exert his supremacy over the Church in England and distance himself from Rome. Describe some of the major differences between the Protestant and Roman Catholic interpretations of Christianity to the children such as the mass, the authority of the Pope and the role of priests and ministers.

Let the children hear you read an extract from the King James Bible in order that they can appreciate the language of the period. Use words that might not be familiar to the children and see if they can find out what they mean. Useful extracts to read would be Genesis, Chapter 1; Psalm 23 and St Matthew's Gospel, Chapter 2.

NB: Interpretations of history are always controversial and elements of religious dispute need to be handled with sensitivity. However, it is important to explore with children the religious disputes of the Tudors and Stuarts as they explain much about the period.

CHAPTER 5

Victorian Britain

This core study unit is designed to introduce children to a period in the past which has left an important legacy to present day Britain. The focus is on people at all different levels of society and how they were affected by industrialisation. This is an ideal topic for study because there is an abundance of physical and literary evidence for children to investigate at first hand. The emphasis here should be on economic developments, public welfare, religion, scientific and cultural achievements and domestic life.

BACKGROUND

The Victorian era (1837–1901) was seen as a time of great stability and prosperity. The early part of the nineteenth century saw Britain emerge as the leading world power. This was largely because Britain underwent industrialisation before any other country in the world. By the time Victoria came to the throne in 1837, steam power had become quite common in industry and the production of raw materials to service the new industries continued at a phenomenal rate. The population also expanded from 14 million in 1827 to 27 million in 1851. Increasing demands for British goods also came from the ever-expanding empire.

Politically, the institutions of government with which we are familiar with today were in place and Victoria rarely involved herself in politics, being content with a largely advisory role. The House of Lords was probably more important then than today as the prime minister could still be chosen from it each year.

Also the House of Commons was still not a very representative place and MPs did little to interfere with the social, political and economic conditions of the time, believing these to be largely ordained by God. The grosser abuses were, however, tackled through the abolition of slavery and the New Poor Law which were passed just before Victoria came to the throne.

By the late 1860s, there had emerged major national politicians such as William Gladstone and Benjamin Disraeli. It was during Gladstone's 'Great Reforming Ministry' between 1868 and 1874 that some of the major reforms were seen. Gladstone sought to find solutions to the Irish question and reformed the Civil Service, army and the Law. An important Education Act was passed in 1870 and the Ballot Act of 1872 introduced secret voting in elections. The subsequent

Disraeli administration was also extensive in its reforming zeal, for example of the Civil Service and the army.

The Victorian period also saw extensive foreign expansion. Prime Minister Palmerston, during the terms 1855–58 and 1859–65, was closely involved in a number of issues including those to do with China and India. Developments in science and learning also meant that exploratory trips to unknown parts of the world were undertaken.

Society itself was changing. Poverty was still the lot of the majority of the population but a new industrial middle class had started to emerge. Many great fortunes were made by

this new class, particularly during the latter part of Victoria's reign.

By the end of the nineteenth century, there had, in addition to all the other changes, been a great expansion in leisure activities, particularly for the poorer classes. Music halls, sport and cheap holidays were now easily available.

The position of women had also begun to change slowly over this period, although more significant reforms would not come until the early years of the twentieth century.

By the time Victoria died in 1901, Britain still held a position of great supremacy in the world, but already new threats, economic, political and military, were developing across the world.

Key dates

1837: Reign of Queen Victoria began. The Chartist Movement introduced the 'People's Charter'.
1842: Mines Act.
1845: Irish potato famine.
1846: Repeal of Corn Laws.
1847: Factory Act – this act reduced the working day to ten hours and limited child employment to the over-eights.
1851: Great Exhibition held.
1845–56: Crimean War.
1857: Indian mutiny.
1859: Charles Darwin published *Origin of Species*.
1861: Death of Prince Albert.
1867: Second Reform Act.
1870: Education Act.
1887: Queen Victoria's Silver Jubilee.
1889: London Dock Strike.
1899–1902: Boer War.
1900: Labour Party founded.
1901: Death of Queen Victoria.

Teaching plan

A series of lessons and activities on Victorian Britain could be structured as follows.
• Victoria and Albert.
• The Industrial Revolution.
• The great reforms of the Victorian era.
• The lives of the poor, the middle class and the rich.
• Britain and the world; empire and exploration.
• Arts, religion and science.
• Victorian education.
• Leisure, entertainment and celebrations in the Victorian era.
• The legacy of the Victorian era.

A topic on the Victorians will allow many opportunities to see aspects of present day British life and society which have been influenced by that era. Additionally, libraries and museums will have many records, documents and artefacts from this period which will allow the children to gain firsthand experience of historical evidence.

ACTIVITIES

1. A poor child

Age range
Seven to nine.

Group size
Individuals or pairs.

What you need
Photocopiable page 176, paper, felt-tipped pens, fabric scraps, adhesive.

What to do
The Victorian period was one of immense poverty for many people. A graphic way to illustrate this is to use a documentary source from the period and let the children build up a picture from what they have heard. The description of the appearance of a poor child on photocopiable page 176 was written in 1861 by Henry Mayhew. Read it to the children and let them work from the sheet to build up a collage picture of the child, following the details of the description as far as possible. Ask them to think about what the description does *not* tell them, for example, the age of the child or his height and weight and encourage them to speculate on other matters such as how he would spend his day, where he would get food to eat, what had happened to his family and so on.

Finally, ask the children to think about how they could acquire more evidence about similar children.

Further activities
Having worked on their own collages, the children could make a life-size collage of the boy. They could also make a life-size collage of a rich Victorian child as a contrast.

You could also use photocopiable page 176 to stimulate imaginative writing and poetry about what life might have been like for poor Victorian children.

2. We are not amused

Age range
Seven to nine.

Group size
Individuals or pairs.

What you need
Period pictures and photographs of Queen Victoria, photographs of other people from the Victorian period.

What to do
The popular image of Queen Victoria has largely been shaped by photographs and illustrations of her. Gather a collection of these together using postcards and reference books. Ask the children to use these photographs as the only source of evidence to describe what they think Queen Victoria must have been like. It is likely that their views will conform to the popular stereotypes.

Show the children photographs of other people and families from the Victorian period and ask them what similarities they can see between these and the pictures of Queen Victoria. It is likely that the children will notice that all the poses are quite formal and that it is very rare for the people to be smiling.

Ask the children to attempt to date the pictures of Queen Victoria. Do they show her in the later stages of her life? Why is this so? How far has the existence of such pictures shaped the popular view of Queen Victoria?

Further activities
Ask the children to collect a series of photographs of the present Royal Family. What do they notice about these photographs compared to the photographs of Queen Victoria and her family? Finally, ask the children to describe what evidence they would need to find out what Queen Victoria was *really* like.

3. Victorian town trail

Age range
Seven to eleven.

Group size
Small groups or the whole class.

What you need
Local history books, modern and Victorian maps of the locality, reference books on the Victorians.

What to do
A useful introduction to a topic on 'The Victorians' is to take the children on a Victorian town trail in order that they can see for themselves evidence from the period. Before the children go out, begin by asking them to do some background work using local history books. What references can they find to the Victorian period? From this work, they can move on to look at more general reference books about the period and see if they can identify any places or sites within their own area which might be from Victorian times.

Clearly, you also need to do some background work in order to direct the outside visit. For some schools, this is not likely to be a problem as the school building itself may date from the Victorian era and be a rich source of inspiration for further study. Other schools might be located in modern housing estates and, therefore, a longer journey will be required to another part of town. However, if it is possible, contact colleagues who work in nearby Victorian schools and ask them if a school exchange could be arranged. The children from the Victorian school could compare aspects of the architecture between their school and the more modern one.

What else should the children look out for during their trail? The following list will provide a few simple guidelines:
• factories;
• houses (both of the poor and the rich);
• street furniture such as lampposts and pillar-boxes;
• shops;
• trades from Victorian times such as blacksmithing and so on.

In addition, contact your local library and ask them if they could display samples of written records, documents and photographs from Victorian times. Local museums, police stations, fire stations and so on, might also have artefacts which the children could be allowed to examine.

During the town trail, ask the children the following questions.
• What do you know about what you have seen?
• Can it be dated accurately?
• Do you have any questions about what you have seen that you cannot answer because there is not sufficient evidence?
• If what they have seen has a modern equivalent, what are the major similarities and differences?

Further activities
Let the children attach a key to a modern wall map of their area which indicates the major Victorian sites of interest. Tell them that this key is to be used by people who want to know more about the Victorians. The children could then prepare a guide book to go with the map.

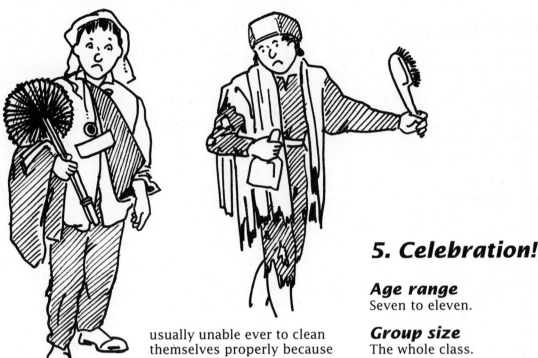

4. Chimney sweep

Age range
Seven to eleven.

Group size
Individuals.

What you need
Descriptions and photographs of chimney sweeps and their child labourers.

What to do
Climbing boys were often apprenticed or, in practice sold for a few shillings, to a chimney sweep. This often happened to boys as young as five or six. Small boys were particularly useful because they could squirm up narrow chimneys. These boys would work up to sixteen hours a day and the mortality rate was very high. Those who survived were beaten and starved and were usually unable ever to clean themselves properly because they were so dirty.

Let the children each write the diary of a chimney sweep's apprentice. They should include in it:
• when they get up in the morning;
• where they live;
• what they have to eat;
• how the chimney sweep treats them;
• what sort of chimneys they sweep;
• who they meet on their travels;
• what sort of illnesses they suffer from;
• how they clean themselves;
• what happens if they try to escape from the chimney sweep or answer him back.

Ask the children to describe what other evidence they might use to help them find out about chimney sweeps.

Further activities
Let the children illustrate their stories and use charcoal to make stains across their writing. They could also make their own chimney models out of card.

5. Celebration!

Age range
Seven to eleven.

Group size
The whole class.

What you need
Period costumes for both adults and children, tables and chairs, hoops, tops and ropes for outdoor games.

What to do
Queen Victoria celebrated her Diamond Jubilee on 22 June 1897. It was a day of great festivity and all schools were given an extra day as holiday for the occasion. A Kent newspaper of the time described what was to happen: '...the children of the various schools shall have Jubilee medals presented to them.... They shall be worn on Tuesday June 22nd.... The children shall march from their different schools and assemble at the cockpit and shall unitedly sing the National Anthem and the Old Hundredth and shall then march round the village and break off near their respective schools, where a tea shall be provided.... There is to be a firework display at 9.30 and a bonfire will be lit at 10 o'clock.

Sports for the children will be arranged.' (From *Bromley Record*, 22 June 1897.)

Arrange your own Diamond Jubilee celebration in school. This would make an excellent ending to a topic on 'Victorian Britain'. If possible try to ensure that the children and adults are appropriately dressed for the occasion. Make up bunting, Jubilee medals, special napkins and so on. The children can then learn some poetry and songs for the occasion as well as the words of the 'National Anthem' and the 'Old Hundredth'. Organise the children so that they march out to the party in lines and present their songs, poetry and music before having a tea party on the school field. Finally, round your day off with sports and games.

Further activity

While the children are preparing for their own special celebration, what can they find out about how the actual Diamond Jubilee was celebrated in their area? Do they have any souvenirs of the event at home such as special plates or thimbles? What can they find out from local newspapers about how the event was celebrated locally? Ask the children what special events they have days off school for.

6. School fees

Age range
Eight to eleven.

Group size
Individuals or pairs.

What you need
Photocopiable page 177, reference books about the Victorians.

What to do
Schooling did not become free until the 1891 Education Act. Photocopiable page 177, derived from a number of sources, describes what a School Board might have charged its pupils. It also provides a conversion table for converting pounds, shillings and pence into decimal currency. However, the children should be made aware that this table only refers to the value of currency immediately prior to decimalisation in 1971 and that, although they can convert the money in this way, the only way to discover the real cost of such education is to compare the cost with what

the average wage was for this time. However, this is something which can be discussed in detail with the children.

Ask the children to work out how much it would have cost for their family to go to school. They could then add up how much income would have to come to the school if all the children in their class had to pay. They will need to become used to working with old money and it might be worth doing some simple sums with the children before starting this activity.

Further activity
What can the children find out about the following aspects of Victorian education?
• Payment by results.
• School boards.
• Ragged schools.

7. Victorian writers

Age range
Eight to eleven.

Group size
Individuals or pairs.

What you need
Novels for children written by Victorian authors such as Lewis Carroll, Anna Sewell, Robert Louis Stevenson and Charles Kingsley.

What to do
Children's novels that were written by Victorian authors are still popular today, but are unlikely to be read in any great numbers by primary-aged children. It is worth introducing them, however, as part of this core study unit because they give an indication of the cultural life of the period. However, they also offer an interesting insight into working conditions, attitudes, domestic life and relationships between different social groups. For example, Charles Kingsley brought the plight of chimney sweeps' climbing boys to public attention.

The following are some suggestions as to how you might use these books if the children are reluctant to read them from cover to cover.

• Read dramatic or amusing extracts from the stories, for example, almost anywhere in *Alice and Wonderland* and the shipwrecking in *Treasure Island*.

• Let the children dramatise the extracts they have heard.

• Watch modern adaptations of these stories on video and ask the children to talk about all the different things they were able to learn about Victorian life.

• Introduce single characters from the different stories, for example Jim Hawkins or Long John Silver, and give some background information about them. Then let the children write their own Victorian adventures involving these characters.

Further activity
Introduce extracts from popular adult books. In particular, what can we learn about Victorian Britain from the stories of Charles Dickens, for example, *Bleak House*, *A Christmas Carol* and *Oliver Twist*. Discuss with the children how far novels and stories can be relied upon to give a true account of what actually happened in the past.

8. Expansion abroad

Age range
Nine to eleven.

Group size
Individuals or pairs.

What you need
A map showing the world in the Victorian period, a modern map of the world, reference books about Victorian explorers.

What to do

The Victorian era was one of exploration and adventure and the expansion of the British Empire. Begin by asking the children why people want to trade overseas or explore and conquer other lands. This is a useful opportunity to talk about the effects of the industrial revolution and how Britain became a producer of all sorts of goods. The children could then look at British colonies which were established during the Victorian period. This issue should be handled with some sensitivity, although it is important that the attitudes of the people at that time are explored and understood. The children should use an atlas to investigate how much of the world was under British control at that stage. They could then compare the names on the Victorian map with the names that now appear on maps.

Finally, ask the children to find out what they can about the journeys of explorers such as Dr David Livingstone, John Speke, Sir Richard Burton and Mary Kingsley. They could trace the journeys of these people on maps of the world.

9. Eating and drinking

Age range
Nine to eleven.

Group size
Individuals or pairs.

What you need
Photocopiable page 178.

What to do
Photocopiable page 178 is an extract taken from Henry Mayhew's *London Labour and the London Poor* (1861) (reprinted 1968, Dover Publications). It describes the weekly income and expenditure of a street cleaner. Give each child a copy of the photocopiable page and ask them to go through it, before they do anything else, and find out what all the words mean. Then you could ask the children the following questions.
• Would it really matter that there was only 10d a week to spare? What else would or could the money be spent on?
• What can you tell about the family's diet?
• Can you make up a week of menus for the man and his family?
• Can you suggest any items on the list that he could do without or is everything a necessity?

Suggest to the children that they take certain items off the list and see if they can work out the new totals. They could use the conversion chart on photocopiable page 178 to help them.

Further activity
Ask the children to compare the items purchased in Victorian times with a typical shopping list of today. They could also compare the prices then and prices today of selected items such as cheese, bacon and tea. This would make an interesting wall display.

10. Victorian schooling

Age range
Ten to eleven.

Group size
The whole class.

What you need
School bell, slate boards and chalk or paper and ink pens, period costume for you and the children.

What to do
In 1880, education was made compulsory for all children aged between five and thirteen.

Recreate a Victorian classroom for the day, using the suggestions that follow.
• Reorganise the layout of the classroom so that the children sit in rows (ideally with more than the normal number of children in the class, as Victorian classes could have as many as 70 or 80 children in them).
• Do not allow any talking unless the children are addressed by the teacher and then they should stand up to give their answers.
• 'Drill' the children in multiplication tables, spelling and reading.
• Give the children handwriting practice using a cursive script.
• Let other children assist with the teaching of reading (the monitorial system).
• Hold 'object' lessons where an object is chosen for discussion and the children are expected to learn any facts taught in the lesson and remember them at a later date. 'Objects' could include an egg, a lion, the sky, winter or trades such as baker or blacksmith.
• See whether the children can recite poems and extracts from the Bible from memory.
• Play outdoor games such as hoops, marbles, skipping and ball games.

This day can be made all the more fun if you and the children wear period costume.

Further activities
Ask the children to explore the responsibility of the School Board. They could imagine that a schools' inspector had visited and not given the school a very good report. What would the School Board do about it?

The children could also consider which elements of Victorian schooling still remain today. Which things did they recognise and which things from the past were very unfamiliar?

CHAPTER 6

Britain since 1930

This core study unit allows children to study a period of history within living memory. By doing this, the connections between the past and the present can be emphasised. The focus of this unit should be placed on major events and developments and on the way of life for different social groups in England, Wales, Scotland and Ireland. In particular, children should be taught about economic developments, the Second World War, social changes, scientific developments, religion and cultural changes.

The six decades that followed the 1930s were ones in which massive social, political, economic and cultural changes took place, as Britain adjusted to playing a lesser role on the world stage and became a much more egalitarian society.

BACKGROUND

The 1930s

The period began with two major themes; the economic situation at home and the rise of Fascism abroad. In 1933, three million people in Britain were unemployed, mainly in areas of the country where traditional, heavy industries were located. Successive governments during the 1930s appeared unable to intervene, and political opposition was largely muted. The British middle classes did, however, begin to prosper as buying their own houses and cars, going on holiday and participating in leisure entertainment all became more popular and affordable. However, for many people the decade was one of dismal poverty. In Germany the Nazis came to power, but throughout the period the majority of politicians in other countries appeared largely unconcerned by the threat. However, by the late 1930s it had become clear that the policy of appeasement had singularly failed, and as a result, Britain went to war against Germany in 1939.

The 1940s

The 1940s were dominated by the Second World War, as Britain, under Winston Churchill, stood alone in Europe against the Nazis. As a consequence British families had to endure many kinds of hardship; air raids, rationing and family separation all became commonplace before Germany was defeated in 1945.

As the war ended a dramatic social change was already underway. A Labour government came to power in Britain and with it came major reconstruction as many industries were brought under public control and the idea of a welfare state was introduced. However, the rest of the decade still proved to be difficult with food rationing being maintained.

The 1950s

In the 1950s, Britain was still trying to emerge from the aftermath of the war. However, 1951 and a Conservative government marked the beginning of a period of relative stability. New housing was built, often in out of town estates, to replace war-damaged homes and new household appliances were introduced on to the market. Entertainment provided by television and cinemas was much more widely available. Abroad, it was clear that Britain's position in the world was declining, and this was demonstrated by such events as the Suez Crisis and the break up of the empire.

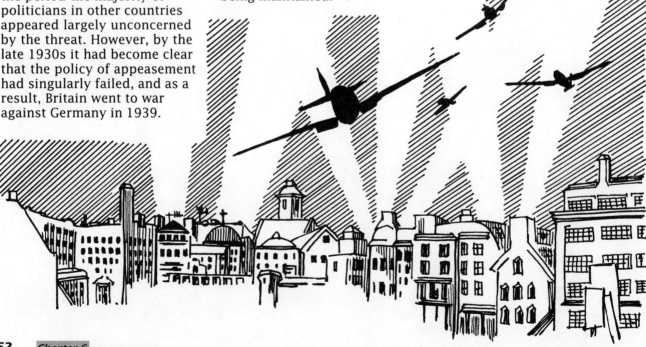

The 1960s

The 1960s marked a major turning point in many aspects of British life. Although the more revolutionary changes of the period affected relatively few people, the new approaches to life and consequent changes in attitudes affected everyone. A Labour government was in power and the period of economic growth and greater prosperity which ensued was shared by many people. However, underlying economic difficulties were never very far away.

In the final analysis, the 1960s will probably be best remembered for the emergence of new ideas and values as 'youth' culture became dominant.

The 1970s

The 1970s began the way it ended, with periods of significant industrial unrest and economic difficulties. The Conservative government of Edward Heath was followed by the Labour administrations of Harold Wilson and James Callaghan. Neither fared particularly well and by the end of the decade serious questions were being raised about education and social policy and how far these had been influenced by the values of the 1960s. In 1979 Margaret Thatcher, Britain's first woman prime minister, was elected. She headed a Conservative government, committed to radical policies.

The 1980s

During the 1980s the country came to be known as 'Thatcher's Britain'. Margaret Thatcher governed with immense force and determination; the power of the unions was curbed, home ownership increased, and many nationalised industries were privatised. However, this encouraged a number of excesses with conspicuous wealth-owning becoming fashionable again and the divisions between rich and poor appearing to be starker than ever.

This decade also saw Britain going to war against Argentina over the issue of the Falkland Islands.

The 1980s were a style and design orientated period. Many of the most publicised businesses of the period were associated with style and fashion. However, by the end of the decade environmental or 'green' issues were becoming increasingly important to the public at large.

The 1990s

The 1990s began with the appointment of a new prime minister, John Major. Mrs Thatcher was deposed by her own party mainly because of her views concerning Britain's role in Europe. John Major's ministerial position was further reinforced by a general election in April 1992 which re-elected him as Prime Minister.

Key dates

1930: Unemployment in Britain passed 2,000,000.
1931: National Government under Ramsey MacDonald was formed.
1936: Edward VIII became king but abdicated later in the year.
1939: War with Germany declared.
1940: Evacuation of British troops from Dunkirk and the Battle of Britain.
1945: The Second World War ended and the first Labour government came to power.
1949: Clothes rationing ended in Britain.
1951: Festival of Britain held.
1953: Coronation of Queen Elizabeth II.
1965: Death penalty abolished in Britain.
1969: British troops sent to Northern Ireland.
1973: Three day working week in Britain.
1975: North Sea oil came on stream for the first time.
1979: Britain's first woman prime minister, Margaret Thatcher, elected.
1982: Britain went to war with Argentina over the Falkland Islands.
1984: Miners strike.
1990: John Major replaced Margaret Thatcher as Prime Minister.
1990–1991: Gulf War.
1992: John Major re-elected as Prime Minister.

Teaching plan

This core study unit lends itself to a decade-by-decade study. Choose one decade to look at in more detail. Beyond that, certain key themes over the period could also be investigated.
• The Second World War;
• Changes in industry and the effects on local communities;
• Social changes;
• Culture and the media.

ACTIVITIES

1. Newspapers: now and then

Age range
Seven to eleven.

Group size
Individuals or pairs.

What you need
Newspapers from today and newspapers from the 1940s and 1950s (replica copies would be suitable).

What to do
Newspapers are a rich source of information about the past. However, they are also useful for providing evidence of how some things change and other things remain the same over time.

Take a selection of newspapers from the 1940s or 1950s and lay them out beside a selection of newspapers from today. Ask the children to look for things that are the same and things that are different between them, giving their initial impressions. They might comment on:
• the titles of newspapers being the same;
• the size of print;
• the use of colour;
• the size of the headlines;
• different styles for broadsheets and tabloids;
• the number of photographs;
• the length of the articles and reports;
• the number and style of advertisements.

When the children have done this, give them a 1940s and 1990s edition of the same newspaper. The children could then look at the features described above, but in particular, they could look for any elements of continuity. For this, they might look at:
• mastheads (the top of the front page of a newspaper);
• columnists and the names used to describe them;
• the organisation of the paper.

Further activity
Could the children visualise what the newspaper might look like in forty or fifty years time? Would it even be in print form? How far has technology affected the style of the newspaper?

2. Fashions

Age range
Seven to eleven.

Group size
Individuals or small groups of three or four.

What you need
A collection of old clothes (brought in from home or borrowed from museums or collections) or photographs and pictures of old clothes, reference books on clothes.

What to do
Clothes are a popular theme to use with children as they provide artefacts which everyone recognises. Encourage the children to bring in collections of old clothes from home. Supplement this by making available reference books, pictures and photographs.

Initially, the children can try to date the clothes, placing them into one of the six decades from the 1930s to the present day. Initially, ask them to do this without using reference books. What clues can they use to help them?

Allow the children to research more about the clothes. What general conclusions can they come to about clothes worn in the later part of this period as compared to the earlier part? Ask the children what conclusions they would draw about a historical period if they had no other evidence than the clothes. Point out to them that this type of evidence must be used with care as it has its limitations, for example:
• clothes are only one part of a whole range of social changes which affect a period;
• the clothes that are kept are often the most interesting and outrageous, rather than everyday clothes worn by most people;
• clothes worn by poorer people are often not retained and cannot therefore be studied in the future.

Further activity
Ask the children to look at one type of clothing over the whole period, such as men's clothes, women's clothes, children's clothes, clothes for sport, uniforms and so on.

3. Parents' time

Age range
Seven to eleven.

Group size
The whole class.

What you need
Photocopiable page 179.

What to do
Parents represent a valuable historical resource for the children and can introduce them to another period in this core study unit. The majority of the children's parents will have been children and teenagers in the late 1960s and 1970s. Concentrate on their early teenage years and ask the children to use photocopiable page 179 to undertake a survey of their parents. Use the results to prepare graphs under each of the headings such as favourite pop stars, favourite television programmes and so on.

In addition, ask the parents
to write or tape record two or
three memories they have
from their teenage years.
These can be used to form
part of a scrapbook, as could
any photographs the parents
are prepared to release.

Make a collection of some of
the artefacts from this period
which the children's parents
may have kept such as
records, posters, stamps,
coins, newspapers, comics and
so on.

End this work by holding a
party in which all the children
(and adults) dress in period
clothes and dance to music
from the period. This history
lesson could even be turned
into quite an effective fund
raiser for the school!

Further activity
If the children have teenage
brothers and sisters they could
compare their experiences
with that of their parents.

4. Television times

Age range
Seven to eleven.

Group size
Individuals or pairs.

What you need
Video recordings of television
programmes from the 1950s to
the 1990s.

What to do
Video recordings now exist for
television programmes from
quite a few years ago. These
can be used as a valuable
historical resource, providing
an insight into aspects of
popular life and culture. It is
worth taking a specific type of
television programme and
looking at it, over a period of
time. Categories could include:
• programmes for pre-school
children;
• children's programmes in
general and specific
programmes which have been

on television for a while such
as *Blue Peter*, *Grange Hill* and
so on;
• light comedy series;
• 'soap' operas that are
popular with the children.

The children need to have a
number of specific things to
look for. First, they can look
for obvious stylistic
differences such as electronic
theme music, the use of
visuals and the type of
presentation. Then they can
look at content. Finally, they
need to assess the information
the programmes give them
about the periods, for
example:
• clothing;
• language;
• the impact of technology;
• general styles such as
haircuts, furniture, cars and so
on.

Further activities
Let the children choose their
favourite programme from the
videos. They can also ask their
parents and grandparents to
describe their favourite
television programmes from
the past and what, in
particular, they remember
about them.

5. Points of view

Age range
Eight to eleven.

Group size
Individuals or pairs.

What you need
Newspapers, reference books, artefacts and other evidence relating to an event since 1930.

What to do
As this core study unit deals with the most recent past, there are many opportunities for children to look at different types of evidence from the same event. This could be handled in one of two ways. First, you could choose an important event of the last 60 years which has been documented in many ways. Obvious examples would be related to the Second World War, for example, the Battle of Britain, Dunkirk, the Blitz and so on. Newspapers, tape and film recordings, photographs, personal accounts, songs, poetry and so on all exist for these sorts of events. The children should build up a picture of the event using all the sources. They need to distinguish between primary sources (accounts from people who lived through the event) and secondary sources (how a reference book has described the event). The children could consider:
• what evidence is missing and what would be needed to build up a fuller picture of the event;
• whether accounts from different people contradict each other;
• whether there is evidence that a 'mythical' element has been introduced to make a certain point (for example the 'spirit' and 'character' of the British people during the Blitz);
• how far the evidence they have is factual and how far it is just a point of view. Is the evidence of someone who was present a fact or is it just a point of view?

The second way to deal with this is to take a contemporary event or even a story which is just breaking and use newspaper coverage, television programmes and children's and adults' perceptions to build up a picture of what has happened. Again, the questions given above could be used.

Additionally, the children could consider the value of, and the dangers in, making instant judgements about an event. What advantages do historians have in looking at an event from a distance? What disadvantages are there in looking at an event from a distance?

The children could make a presentation based on the work they have carried out. If other adults and children are invited to see it, how far are their perceptions the same?

6. War is declared

Age range
Eight to eleven.

Group size
Individuals.

What you need
Extract from Neville Chamberlain's declaration of war on behalf of Britain.

What to do
One of the most dramatic moments in the history of Britain this century was when Neville Chamberlain announced Britain's declaration of war on Germany. Read the following extract to the children or better still, play them a recording of Chamberlain speaking:

'I am speaking to you from the Cabinet Room at 10, Downing Street.

This morning the British Ambassador in Berlin handed the German Government a

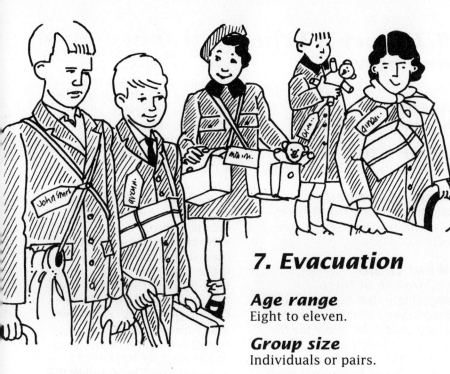

7. Evacuation

Age range
Eight to eleven.

Group size
Individuals or pairs.

What you need
Map of Britain, reference books about the period, an adult who was evacuated during the war.

What to do
Evacuation was a wartime reality for many thousands of children in Britain. It is an experience which modern day children find hard to comprehend and so, if possible, begin by helping the children to understand why children were evacuated, where from and where to.

Tell the children to look at a map of Britain and suggest places which they think would make good evacuation sites. Why do they think these are good places? Ask them what they would take with them if they were evacuated and were only allowed to take one suitcase.

If possible, try to invite an adult who was evacuated during the war to talk to the children. The children should each prepare a question to ask,

for example:
• 'Where did you live and where were you evacuated to?'
• 'Who did you stay with?'
• 'What did you have to do that you had never done before?'
• 'Did you hear from your parents much?'
• 'How did you know what was happening to them?'
• 'What happened to your schoolwork and education?'

Further activities
Can the children make contact with anyone who looked after evacuated children during the war? Can they imagine what the difficulties would have been for a child from the city living in the country?

8. Patterns of employment

Age range
Nine to eleven.

Group size
Individuals.

What you need
Photocopiable page 180, reference books about industry in the 1930s and today.

What to do
Any study of 'Britain since 1930' needs to look at the changing patterns of employment and how specific industries have grown and declined over the period. Photocopiable page 180 consists of two maps of Britain. The children will need to research what Britain's major industries were in the 1930s and what they are now. In particular, they could look at:

final note stating that unless we heard from them by 11 o'clock that they were prepared to withdraw their troops from Poland a state of war would exist between us.

I have to tell you that no such undertaking has been received and consequently this country is at war with Germany.'

Ask the children for their immediate response to this extract. How do they think people of the time would have felt? Would there have been different reactions from different people? Ask the children to imagine that they are a parent writing to their soldier son immediately after they have heard this announcement. What would they say in their letters?

Further activity
Ask the children to use reference books to find out what happened in the first few months of war, before major hostilities began.

- coal mining;
- shipbuilding;
- steel manufacturing;
- machine-tool manufacturing;
- chemical industry;
- food;
- service industries;
- high technology industries.

The children could design symbols for each of the major industries and put them on the map. They could then write two or three sentences about each industry on the back of the sheet.

The children could look at where particular industries were located in the early part of the period. They will notice that areas which were accessible by sea were often major producers of raw materials or products associated with raw materials. Why was this the case? Can the children consider what the effects might have been in areas where heavy industries have declined?

Further activities
Ask the children to look in depth at one particular industry associated with their area. What has happened to it over the period? They could also conduct an industrial survey of their area. Which industries were previously major employers but now no longer exist? Which industries did not exist ten or twenty years ago but have appeared in the interim? The children could also look at the effects of unemployment in their area – although this does need to be handled with sensitivity.

9. History is here and now

Age range
Nine to eleven.

Group size
Small groups of three or four.

What you need
Materials which the children identify for themselves (see below).

What to do
Children often fail to appreciate that history is being made every minute. This core study unit does allow for the study of contemporary history and, in particular, it introduces the problems historians have in explaining a period of history. Ask each group to select five items which they believe would be of interest to an historian wanting to find out as much as he or she can about 'Britain in the 1990s', a hundred years from now. Allow each group a few minutes to describe what their items are and why they think they would be of particular interest to an historian. In evaluating the children's choices and encouraging others to ask questions, use the following 'prompt' list:

- Is the selection of items very specific to a particular day or week, for example, a newspaper or the number one record in the charts? If it is, does this represent widely enough a range of happenings? Or, is providing a 'snapshot' the best approach?
- Does the selection of items represent the lives of one specific group, for example, boys, girls or one specific ethnic group?
- What questions would be left unanswered about the period if the historian of the future only had the five items or all the items of all the groups in the class? Clearly, there are many questions, but do they represent a fundamental gap in knowledge that could have been rectified by a more judicious selection?

Further activity
Local history societies are often aware of 'time capsules' which have been buried in their area. Find out what kinds of things lie buried in your locality.

CHAPTER 7

Ancient Greece

This core study unit is designed to introduce children to the civilisation of Ancient Greece. It also offers opportunities for the children to see what contribution Ancient Greece has made to modern society. The focus should be on the way of life, beliefs and technological achievements of the Ancient Greeks. In particular, the children should learn about the city state, the economy, everyday life, religion and thought, the arts, relations with other peoples and the legacy of Ancient Greece.

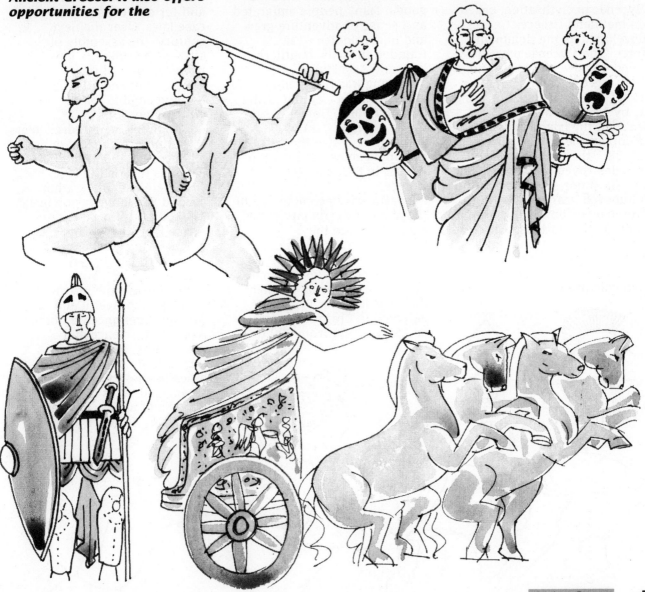

BACKGROUND

The story of Ancient Greece spans just under 2000 years. It began around 2000BC when tribes from Russia settled in Greece and mixed with the indigenous population. It was from this mixture that the Greek language developed. From 1600BC, and for the next four hundred years, the Mycenaean civilisation, based on mainland Greece, developed as the dominant force. The Mycenaeans were ruled by powerful kings and were a great trading people. Their power extended to Crete as by 1450BC they had invaded the island and occupied the palaces there. In 1200BC, the Greeks attacked and destroyed the city of Troy in Asia Minor. However, within a hundred years of this, the Mycenaeans power was on the wane as the Dorians, who were Greek speakers from the north, invaded Greece. By 1500BC Mycenaean civilisation had collapsed.

Throughout Greece, during this period, a number of city states developed. Essentially, city states were free-standing political entities grouped around a centre of population. Trade grew as new goods were manufactured and city states realised that they could not be self-sufficient in all their goods. Many people emigrated as a sense of adventure grew and new colonies were founded in Sicily, southern Italy and Asia Minor.

Writing was flourishing along with the city states and around 800BC, Homer is said to have composed the *Iliad* and *Odyssey*. Also the first Olympic games were held in 776BC, in Ells, southern Greece.

Sparta was becoming one of the most powerful city states, expanding into the Peloponnese and Messenia between 700BC and 500BC.

As the city states became ever more powerful, so then did their leaders. Tyrants emerged in Corinth, Megara and Sicyon and from 700 to

600BC there were a number of revolts. Conquered people were forced into slavery and it was following a slave revolt that the Spartans became full-time soldiers.

By 510BC Athens had become a democracy. In such a democracy all citizens (free males) were allowed to vote and juries were set up to try case laws. Over the next century, the assembly of citizens became the most powerful part of the government and all citizens became eligible for all government jobs.

The following hundred years were times of shifting military alliances. In 490BC the Persians invaded Greece, but were defeated at Marathon. A second Persian invasion began in 480BC but the city states formed an alliance and defeated the invaders in a naval battle in the Bay of Salamis.

In contrast, the next fifty years were peaceful and Athens experienced a Golden Age of art, science and philosophy, becoming increasingly powerful with 265 cities paying tribute to it. This meant that taxes in the form of goods and money had to be paid to it. However, this

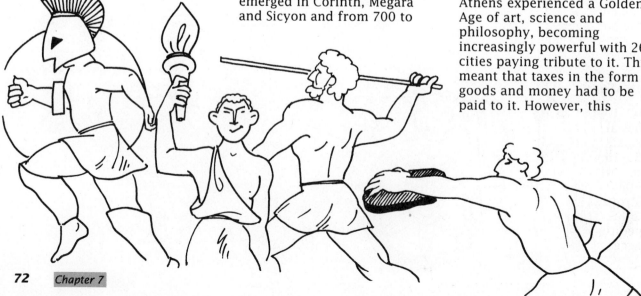

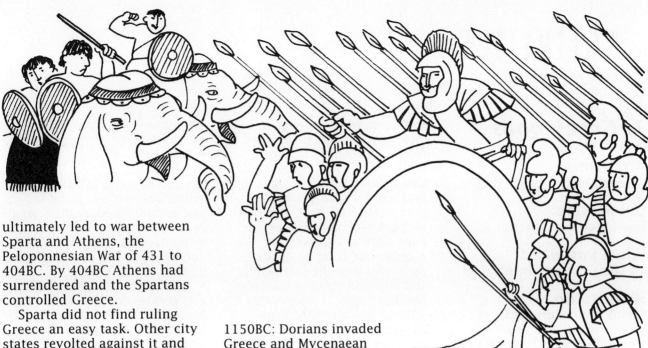

ultimately led to war between Sparta and Athens, the Peloponnesian War of 431 to 404BC. By 404BC Athens had surrendered and the Spartans controlled Greece.

Sparta did not find ruling Greece an easy task. Other city states revolted against it and eventually Philip of Macedonia made himself master of Greece following the Battle of Chaironeia in 338BC. He was succeeded by his son, Alexander, who invaded Persia and eventually conquered an empire which ran from Egypt to India.

Following the death of Alexander in 323BC, the empire divided into three parts; Macedonia, Asia Minor and Egypt. Macedonia sought to dominate, but by 146BC the Romans had conquered the Greek cities and by 145BC, Rome had combined the Greek cities so that they made up the province of Macedonia.

Key dates

2000–1900BC: Greek speaking tribes arrived from western Russia.
1650–1450BC: Plycenans dominated Greece.
1450BC: Cretan civilisation destroyed.
1220BC: Troy destroyed by expedition from mainland Greece.

1150BC: Dorians invaded Greece and Mycenaean civilisation collapsed.
900–750BC: City states emerged.
776BC: First Olympic Games held.
750BC: The *Iliad* and *Odyssey*, by Homer, believed to have been written.
700–500BC: Sparta came to dominate Peloponnese.
507BC: Athenian democracy began.
490–479BC: Persian wars.
477–405BC: Athens became dominant power.
431–404BC: Peloponnesian War between Athens and Sparta.
365–338BC: Philip of Macedonia ruled Greece.
336BC: Alexander succeeded his father Philip on his death.
336–323BC: Alexander came to dominate an empire stretching from Egypt to north India.
323BC: Alexander (the Great) died, aged 32.
323–280BC: Empire broken up into Macedonia, Asia Minor and Egypt.
280–197BC: Greek city states revolted against, and eventually defeated, Macedonia, with the assistance

of the Romans, at the battle of Cynoscephalae in 197BC.
146BC: Greek cities rose against the domination of Rome, but were defeated at the Battle of Corinth.
145BC: Rome combined the Greek cities into the province of Macedonia.

Teaching plan

A series of lessons and activities on Ancient Greece could be planned as follows.
• A time span of 2000 years: the glory of Ancient Greece (including in-depth studies of key characters such as the Mycenaeans, Spartans, Philip and Alexander).
• Gods, myths and legends.
• Life in a city state.
• States at war.
• Festivals and the theatre.
• The Olympic Games.
• Science, the arts and philosophy.
• The legacy of Ancient Greece.

ACTIVITIES

1. Greek gods

Age range
Seven to eleven.

Group size
Small groups of three or four.

What you need
No special requirements.

What to do
Divide the children into groups of three or four and give each group the name of a Greek god. Ask them to create a picture of what they think the god looks like and then tell them to write and perform a story involving this god.

Twelve Greek gods became more important than the rest and these were believed to live on Mount Olympus. Each had their own special sign or symbol and the children could also devise their own signs or symbols for their gods and then try to find out the correct sign for each god. The twelve gods were as follows:

• Zeus – the ruler of all the gods who sent the rain, wind and dew and was the master of thunder;
• Hera – third wife of Zeus who protected wives and mothers;
• Athena – daughter of Zeus and the goddess of wisdom;
• Apollo – son of Zeus and the god of light, music, healing and sudden death;
• Artemis – twin sister of Apollo and a goddess of light, protecting girls and virgins;

• Hermes – the son of Zeus, the messenger of the gods;
• Ares – son of Zeus and hated by all the other gods. He was the god of war and blind, brutal destruction, going to war accompanied by his sons Fear and Fright;
• Hephaestus – the son of Zeus and the lame blacksmith of the gods;
• Aphrodite – a cousin of Zeus and goddess of love and gardens;
• Poseidon – a brother of Zeus who lost the battle for the sky and became the god of the sea and air;
• Hestia – older sister of Zeus, the calm goddess of household fire and the public hearth;
• Demeter – sister of Zeus and the goddess of the fruitful earth.

Further activity
Ask the children to consider the role played by gods in Greek society.

2. Chiton

Age range
Seven to eleven.

Group size
Individuals.

What you need
Lengths of plain cloth of an appropriate size for the children to wear as chitons.

What to do
Greek clothes were extremely simple and easy to wear. No underclothes were worn, just a piece of cloth pinned and tied to make a tunic called a chiton. Another piece of cloth would be draped over it as a cloak. Young men and slaves wore short chitons; women and older men wore longer ones. The chitons had no pockets. Let the children dress as Greeks, using the pieces of cloth to make chitons. There were two ways of putting on a chiton.
• Fold over a third of the cloth twice, pin it at the shoulders and tie a belt over or under the flap of cloth.
• Fold the cloth and pin along the top. Tie in two places and pull out the cloth between the belts.

Further activity
Ask the children to investigate further about Greek clothes and how they were made. They could also look at hairstyles and jewellery of the period.

3. The ancient Olympics

Age range
Seven to eleven.

Group size
The whole class and other classes in the school.

What you need
Reference books about the ancient and modern Olympics, sports equipment to enable the children to carry out the events described below, Greek-style costumes.

What to do
Begin by letting the children research the ancient Olympics. They should find out such things as where and when they were held, who took part in them and so on. Having carried out their research the children can hold their own ancient Olympics. They can dress up in Greek costumes and other classes can join in, representing different city states. Choose teams to participate in each of the five events of the Pentathlon:
• the foot race;
• discus throwing;
• long jump;
• javelin throwing (this could be substituted by throwing a cricket ball);
• wrestling (this could be substituted by holding a relay race).

Begin the games by having a messenger take a scroll to each of the classes or city states inviting them to participate. Each class should bring with them to the games an item for the altar of Zeus. The spectators could have olive branches made out of card and winners can be presented with simple olive wreaths and given a hero's welcome in their 'city state'. Finally, the games could end with feasting and drinking in honour of Zeus.

Further activity
Ask the children to investigate the modern Olympic games and find out which elements of the Greek games have survived today. Tell them to find out, in particular, why the marathon race is popularly associated with the ancient Olympics although no such event took place.

4. Greek theatre

Age range
Seven to eleven.

Group size
Small groups of three or four.

What you need
Greek costumes, masks for the children (could be made out of paper or papier mâché), reference books about Greek theatre.

What to do
Greek theatre developed out of religious festivals, although over time plays as we know them today also began to emerge.

Introduce the children to the three main types of Greek play:
• tragedies: with serious themes, often involving 'sacrifice', where an individual sacrificed his own happiness for the common good;
• satyr plays: written by the same authors who wrote the tragedies and they made fun of the legends;
• comedies: boisterous and often vulgar, poking fun at gods and men.

Ask the children to write a short play in each of the above styles. They could use as themes:
• war with the Spartans;
• the Olympics;
• the gods and how they might intervene in human life;
• aspects of Greek myths and legends.

The children could then make masks appropriate to the plays and perform them to the rest of the class.

Further activities
Ask the children to find out more about myths and legends of the Ancient Greeks which they could use to perform in their theatre. Look at:
• Jason and the golden fleece;
• Aesop's fables;
• the Trojan War;
• the *Odyssey* and the *Iliad*.

This allows for a discussion on what is true in history and what is myth or legend. Finally, the children can look at elements of modern theatre which have been influenced by the Greeks.

5. Forms of government

Age range
Eight to eleven.

Groups size
The whole class.

What you need
No special requirements.

What to do
During the time of Ancient Greece, there were various forms of government. These were as follows:
• Monarchy: where the king ruled alone or with a small council of important men.
• Tyranny: which was rule by a man who took power by force.
• Aristocracy: where the nobles governed and passed this responsibility on to their sons.
• Oligarchy: which was rule by a few, usually those who owned property.

• Democracy: all male citizens shared in lawmaking (women, slaves and children were not counted as citizens).

Ask the children to consider each form of government in turn. You could even let the class experience each of the different forms of government for part of the day. Which do they prefer? What are the advantages and disadvantages of each form of government? Ask the children to consider whether they think that different kinds of government were better suited for different periods of Greek history. Look at the reasons why women and slaves were excluded from government.

Further activity

You might also like to consider, with the children, current-day democracy in Britain. In what ways is it similar to the democracy of the Greeks? In what ways is it different? Encourage the children to think particularly about:
• representative democracy as opposed to direct democracy;
• the role of women;
• political parties.

6. The Greek alphabet

Age range
Eight to eleven.

Group size
Individuals.

What you need
Photocopiable page 181.

What to do
Photocopiable page 181 shows the Greek alphabet, together with the names of the letters and how they are pronounced in English. Ask the children to write English words in Greek. They might like to start by writing their names. They could also look at some Greek words and see if they can translate them into English.

The page also contains English words which have Greek origins. Using a dictionary, ask the children to find out what the Greek element of the word is and what it means.

Further activity
Let the children look at English words which originate from other languages such as Latin, French and American English.

7. Life in Sparta

Age range
Eight to eleven.

Group size
Individuals.

What you need
Reference books describing life in Sparta.

What to do
Life in most city states was very similar apart from in Sparta, where all citizens (free men over the age of 20) were full-time soldiers. The reason for this was to keep the slaves or helots (serfs) under control. At the age of seven, a Spartan boy would leave his mother and go to live in the mountains. There he would exercise and be trained in all aspects of warfare. A Spartan male could marry at the age of 20, but he still had to eat, live and sleep at his regimental barracks until he was 30.

Ask the children to imagine that they are young Spartans taken away from home to train as soldiers. Encourage them to describe what things they do, what they eat and where they live. They could also describe their feelings about such a life and their feelings towards the helots and slaves.

Further activities
Tell the children to investigate the Spartans in more detail. How were their towns organised? What was the relative sizes of Spartan and helot dwellings? Can the children find out how the word 'spartan' is used today?

8. Time frame

Age range
Nine to eleven.

Group size
Individuals or pairs.

What you need
Photocopiable page 182, reference books with time-lines or information relating to the period 2000BC to AD1.

What to do
Of all the core study units the Ancient Greeks covers the most extensive period of time. Children will find it hard to appreciate that the story of Ancient Greece covers a period of time as long as that between the birth of Christ and the present day. However, in order to give them some idea of the development of human history, photocopiable page 182 outlines the key events in Greek history and challenges the children to find out what other things were happening during this period. The children will need to use a series of reference books to find the information necessary to compete the chart. It is important to stress to them that although the emphasis is on the history of Ancient Greece during this period, the histories of other people are equally valuable, if less well-known.

Further activity
Ask the children to consider the contribution made by modern communications in building up a picture of what is going on in all parts of the world. When did such information first become available?

9. Greek architecture

Age range
Nine to eleven.

Group size
Individuals or pairs.

What you need
Reference books on Greek architecture, graph paper, pencils, ruler, cardboard tubes, boxes, polystyrene tiles, paints, adhesives, scissors.

What to do
There were two main styles of Greek architecture, the Doric and the Ionic. The Doric style was simple and severe. In a Doric temple, the columns rose straight from the floor to a simple capital.

The Ionic style came from the Greek cities of Asia Minor and was much more decorative and delicate than the Doric. The columns were taller and slimmer and at the base was a decorated plinth, at the top a carved, scrolled capital.

From the fifth century BC, the Corinthian style of capital decoration incorporating scrolls and sprays of acanthus leaves became popular.

Ask the children to use reference books to find illustrations of these styles. The children could then draw their own Greek temples based on each of the three styles. Can they turn these illustrations into three-dimensional models? They could use cardboard tubes for the columns, long narrow boxes to form the beams across the top and a polystyrene tile for the section above the beams.

Further activity
Ask the children to find illustrations of modern buildings which are based on the Greek style. Why do they think that people today would wish to design modern buildings in Greek style?

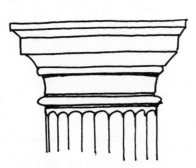

CHAPTER 8

Exploration and encounters 1450 to 1550

This core study unit looks at the developments which brought European nations into contact with American peoples. The focus should be on the reasons for exploration, the nature of the Aztec civilisation and the encounter between two cultures and its results.

The age of discovery, when Europeans set out across the world, began in the fifteenth century. Their motivation was partly economic, seeking new lands with whom to trade, and also religious. There was a great desire to spread Christianity throughout the world. Essentially however, the journeys were motivated by a spirit of exploration and a desire for discovery.

BACKGROUND

The most important explorer at the end of the fifteenth century was Christopher Columbus, an Italian who settled in Portugal. He was encouraged and supported in his explorations by Queen Isabella of Spain. The Portuguese had refused to back his plan to reach the East Indies by sailing west. Up until then, the Portuguese had always sailed east, which meant that first they had to sail a long way south. Columbus believed that the world was round and he therefore believed that if he sailed west he would still arrive at the Indies but from the opposite direction. What Columbus did not know about however, was the existence of the Americas. When he landed in the Caribbean islands 1492, he was certain that he had arrived in the East Indies of Asia. Indeed, right up until the time he died, Columbus refused to accept that he had discovered a new continent, although other explorers were beginning to realise that he had.

In the early sixteenth century, the Spanish began to look for new lands to add to their empire. In 1519,

Hernando Cortés, the Spanish governor of Cuba, led a small army of men into the Mexican interior where there was rumoured to be a rich city. Initially, the Spaniards were treated as gods by Montezuma and his Aztec people. The Aztec civilisation was one of great splendour and achievement, but it was also ruled by a superstitious man who often acted with barbarity. Although Cortés was finally driven out of Mexico because of his cruelty and use of force, he soon returned with large forces and the Aztecs were slaughtered, and their civilisation ransacked.

This period of exploration also saw the first circumnavigation of the world by Ferdinand Magellan. However, exploring by sea remained very hazardous. Many sailors and explorers died in primitive living conditions where food was simple and scarce. Disease was an ever present threat and yet these hardships did not appear to deter the ambitions of empires and individuals.

Key dates

1492: Columbus discovered the West Indies.
1493: Columbus' second voyage to the New World.
1498: Columbus' third voyage to the New World.
1519: Hernando Cortés reached the Aztec civilisation which was ruled by King Montezuma. First circumnavigation of the world by Ferdinand Magellan.
1521: Siege of the Aztec city of Tenochtitlan ended in Spanish domination.

Teaching plan

A series of lessons and activities on exploration and encounters could be organised as follows.
• The life and travels of Christopher Columbus.
• Life on board a ship.
• Magellan and the circumnavigation of the world.
• The expansion of the Spanish Empire.
• The Aztecs.

ACTIVITIES

1. The Santa Maria

Age range
Seven to nine.

Group size
Individuals.

What you need
Photocopiable page 183, reference books about the period.

What to do
Photocopiable page 183 shows a cross section of the *Santa Maria*, Columbus' ship. It had an upper or main deck and a quarter deck on which were situated the helm and the captain's cabin. There was also a small foredeck, which was used as a storeroom, and a hold where the food and cargo were stored.

The photocopiable page also lists various different parts of the ship. Can the children decide where these various things might go and draw them in? They could then use reference books to see how far they were correct in where they positioned the different items.

Further activity
Ask the children to find out about other famous ships of the period such as the *Pinta*, the *Nina*, the *Victoria* and the *Santiago*.

2. The crew of the Santa Maria

Age range
Seven to eleven.

Group size
Individuals.

What you need
Dictionary.

What to do
A ship like the *Santa Maria* would have a crew of approximately forty men, a number of whom would have had specialist functions. Give the children the list below and see if they can describe, with the aid of a dictionary if necessary, what all these different people would have had to do:
• captain;
• mate;
• pilot;
• interpreter;
• lawyer;
• secretary of the fleet;
• king's officer;
• boatswain;
• surgeon;
• storekeeper;
• carpenter;
• cooper;
• caulker;
• ship's boy;
• ordinary sailor.

Further activities
Can the children find out what size of crew there is on a modern naval ship? Are any jobs still the same? Are there new jobs on a modern ship? Would a modern ship still have people like coopers and caulkers on it?

3. Life on board

Age range
Seven to eleven.

Group size
Individuals.

What you need
Reference books about the period.

What to do
The children should imagine that they are the ship's captain of the *Santa Maria* writing up the log book in 1492. What sort of things might they say? They could comment on:
• relationships with Christopher Columbus and what demands he was making;
• the state of weather;
• the condition of the ship and crew;
• any punishments handed out;
• land sited or seen;
• work done during the day.

Further activity
Ask the children to write an account of life on board ship from the point of view of an ordinary sailor. Are there things that the ordinary sailor might say that the captain would not comment on?

4. Aztec masks

Age range
Seven to eleven.

Group size
Individuals.

What you need
Card, scissors, adhesive, gold coloured self-adhesive paper, reference books about the Aztecs.

What to do
The Aztecs made masks for religious festivals. The children could research what these masks looked like and then make their own from card. They could then decorate them using the gold self-adhesive paper.

Further activity
Religion was very important to the Aztecs. In particular, they believed that the gods had decided what would happen to each person before they had been born. Additionally, the Aztecs believed that the world had lived through the destruction of four suns before coming to the present, fifth sun. Although the Aztecs had their own explanations for the destruction of each of the suns, the children could write their own Aztec myth based on the destruction of the suns.

5. Foods from afar

Age range
Seven to eleven.

Group size
Individuals or pairs.

What you need
Examples of produce which was discovered in the fifteenth and sixteenth centuries, for example, maize, tomatoes, strawberries, peppers, avocado, pineapple, cinnamon and nutmeg.

What to do
A lot of food products which we now take for granted were new to Columbus and other explorers of the period. Lay out a sample of each of the above items and ask the children to write descriptions of them as if this was the first time they had ever seen and tasted the product. (You must, of course, be sensitive to any food allergies you are aware of. If in any doubt, consult parents in advance of undertaking this activity.) They should describe their colour, texture, smell and taste. Ask the children to swap their descriptions with a friend who must try to identify which item is being described.

Further activity
Ask the children to find out which of the products described above are now grown in this country and which are still only grown in the country in which they were discovered. They can then make a food map of the world.

6. Pictograms

Age range
Seven to eleven.

Group size
Pairs.

What you need
Strong brown paper, inks.

What to do
The Aztecs had no formal script for writing. Instead, they used pictograms which consisted of little pictures to represent words. Ask the children to discuss the advantages and disadvantages of this kind of communication. Then, they can try and write a simple message for each other using only pictograms and a limited number of words.

The children could then draw Aztec pictograms on to brown paper using inks.

Further activity
Can the children think of other kinds of communication that do not depend on a written script?

7. Religious influences

Age range
Nine to eleven.

Group size
Individuals or pairs.

What you need
No special requirements.

What to do
Discuss with the children the role that religion played in motivating people to explore abroad. Encourage them to look at the influence of the church and the injunctions of Christ, contained in the Bible, in particular.

During explorations when on board ship, the day always began with a hymn sung by one of the ship's boys. A boy also sang at the evening service and it was his duty to turn the sand glasses which measured the time. A religious chant would follow the turning of the glasses:

The watch is called
The glass floweth
We shall make a good voyage
If God willeth.

Ask the children to make up their own religious chants for jobs that would be done on ship such as keeping lookout, cooking the dinner, scrubbing the decks and so on.

Further activity
Tell the children to consider how far religion has been an influence in twentieth-century voyages of exploration. This could be compared with the Victorian era.

CHAPTER 9

Supplementary study unit A

The intention of the six themes in this study unit is to provide units which involve studying a theme over a longer period of time. These themes introduce the study of important historical issues over a span of time which lasts for at least one thousand years. Additionally, the children should be able to compare, through the study of these themes, developments in different periods and show links between local, British, European and world history.

The focus of the first theme is on the design of the ships, economic aspects of shipping, seafaring and science; politics, seafaring, ships and society. The second theme looks at farming methods, food production and farming. The intention of the third theme is to explore how buildings can tell us about the way people lived in the past – focusing on construction, the function of buildings and the design of buildings. The fourth theme is intended to let children see the importance of writing and printing in history by looking at methods of writing and printing and the growth of literacy. This is done by looking at specifically contrasting periods in history. The focus of the fifth theme is the development of transport in the context of technological developments and the environment, and the economic and social consequences of transport developments. The final theme introduces children to the home and family life of specific past societies with the focus being on the similarities and differences between periods. In particular the children could consider the development of the family, household economics, daily life in households, families and ritual, and household interiors.

BACKGROUND

Ships and seafarers

The first historical evidence of seafaring comes from Ancient Egypt almost three hundred years before the birth of Christ. Within five hundred years, the Egyptians were sailing great distances in ships which had masts and oars.

Subsequent developments before the birth of Christ saw ships adapted for warfare, as both the Greeks and Romans utilised ships for this purpose. Great sea battles followed, such as the Battle of Salamis in 480BC when the Greeks defeated the Persians. Both the empires of Greece and Rome also made extensive use of ships for trade and the transporting of goods.

Over the next 750 to 800 years, there were few significant developments in the history of seafaring. However, the Vikings changed all that. For over 250 years, their elegantly designed longships took warriors and traders all across the world. Viking ships and seafarers became well known and were depicted on many objects made by both the invaders and the invaded. Viking ships were clinker-built from overlapping planks and this style continued to be used throughout the Middle Ages, although by the thirteenth century both the stern and the bow had become more 'castle-like' in shape.

Technological developments such as the stern rudder and the magnetic compass in the fifteenth century also allowed traders to travel more quickly so that they could meet the demand caused as the city states, such as Venice and Genoa, extended their trade.

The period between 1450 and 1600 was a golden age for ships and seafarers as explorers extended people's knowledge of the known world. Military conquest, economic expansion, Christian mission and a sense of

adventure all contributed to a new spirit. Christopher Columbus was the most famous adventurer of the period. He crossed the Atlantic Ocean in 1492 and discovered the islands of the West Indies.

In the sixteenth century, the trips of exploration were continued by sailors such as Francis Drake. This was also the period when purpose-built, offensive warships were originated. Henry VIII built warships that were armed with batteries of cannons. Ultimately, however, one of the great events of the period, the sailing of the Spanish Armada, proved that the tactics of sailors were as important as the structures of ships.

By the eighteenth century, as British trade expanded through companies such as the British East India Company, merchant ships were large and sophisticated. They were also designed to repel attacks by pirates, a common threat in the period, and not surprising, given the valuable cargoes which were being carried. The history of shipping in this period would not be complete without a reference to the slave trade. Ships would sail out of England and France with products such as cotton goods to trade in the Caribbean in exchange for slaves. The conditions for slaves on board ships were appalling and many died on the trips back to Europe. Eventually, through campaigns led by people such as William Wilberforce, the slave trade was made illegal in 1807 in Britain, although it still continued for many years.

The major European wars at the beginning of the nineteenth century were largely fought at sea as Britain triumphed over the French in 1805 and 1815. The growth of the British Empire during the rest of the century was also largely attributable to ships and seafarers.

The history of shipping was to change for ever with the advent of steam power. The first Atlantic crossing by a sailing ship fitted with a steam engine was made by the *Savannah* in 1819.

Ships and sailors continued to be intimately associated with war in general as the century dragged on. This was because control of the seas often brought significant military advantage and was important in the control of trade. Battleships started to be made from iron and the twentieth century saw the building of huge ships, pleasure liners and merchant vessels as well battleships.

The twentieth century also saw the development of submarine and hovercraft technology and the use of boats for sport and leisure. Faster communications and travel by other means, such as air, meant that ships were no longer the only way to travel a long distance.

Key dates

*c.*3400BC: First pictures of papyrus and wooden boats in Egypt.

*c.*2400BC: First pictures of ships used for military purposes; for example, the Pharaoh Sature's raid on the Syrian coast.

480BC: Battle of Salamis between the Greeks and Persians.

AD350–500: The Angles and Saxons invaded Britain by ship.

875–1000: Viking longboats and warriors terrorised the known world.

1290: Marco Polo reported seeing large Chinese passenger-carrying merchant junks.

1488–9: Bartholomew Diaz found a sea route to India.

1492: Christopher Columbus crossed the Atlantic.

1497: John Cabot reached the coast of Newfoundland.

1511: Henry VIII built the warships *Mary Rose* and *Great Harry*.

1519–22: Ferdinand Magellan was the first European to cross the Pacific.

1588: The Spanish Armada was defeated by the English.

1620: Pilgrim Fathers set sail on the *Mayflower* from Plymouth to America.

1768–71: James Cook discovered New Zealand.

1802: The world's first working steamboat, *Charlotte Dundas*, was built.

1819: *Savannah* crossed the Atlantic under sail with a small steam engine.

1869: *Cutty Sark* built.

1906: British cruiser *Dreadnought* transformed battleship design.

1912: Sinking of the *Titanic*.

1914–18: Submarines played a major part in First World War.

1941: Attack on Pearl Harbour.

1955: USS *Nautilus* became the world's first nuclear-powered submarine.

1982: Falklands War led to significant use of missile technology in sea wars.

Teaching plan

A series of lessons and activities on 'Ships and seafarers' could be organised as follows.

• The earliest ships and seafarers;

• Invasion! Ships in Greek, Roman and Viking times;

• A life at sea – the lives of sailors through time;

• From paddle to submarine – the history of the technology of shipping;

• Pirates!

• Ships of war;

• The slave trade;

• Ships for trade;

Links could also be made with Core Study Units 1, 2, 3, 5 and 6.

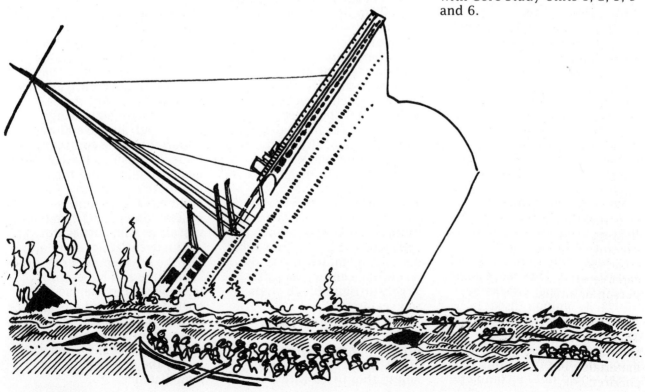

ACTIVITIES

1. Crossing water

Age range
Seven to nine.

Group size
Small groups of three or four.

What you need
Pieces of wood, paper, leather, straw, tank of water.

What to do
People first learned about travelling on water by a process of trial and error. Ask the children why people would have wanted to go on to water in the first place. The children can then experiment with different materials to see which float on their own and what effect this might have. They should record their findings and use them to design and make a boat-like structure, made from materials which early people would have used. Do not let them attach the wood together with nails. Instead ask them to find other ways of binding the materials together.

When finished, their structures must be capable of floating a set distance, for example, a metre without collapsing and must be capable of supporting a play person or animal.

Further activity
This activity could be extended as far as the materials available allow. The children could also be asked to make a boat with a sail which would be capable of floating in water outside. Or they could be given materials such as twine or raffia, which are similar to river reeds and be asked to bind them together in a way which would float, for example, for a minute. Finally, tell the children to investigate the different sources of information available about the earliest boats.

2. A Greek galley

Age range
Seven to eleven.

Group size
Individuals.

What you need
Clay or self hardening modelling material, modelling paints suitable for clay, reference books about Ancient Greece or the history of ships.

What to do
Much of our evidence about Greek ships comes from drawings and paintings on Greek pottery. Ask the children to find out about Greek war galleys.
• How long were they?
• What did they carry on board?
• What was life like on board?
• How did they move?
• How many men did they carry?

Ask the children to make a piece of clay into a fairly flat, irregular shape and fire it or leave it to harden. The children can then paint on to it a picture of part of a war galley as if the clay had come from a piece of Greek pottery which had been broken.

Further activity
Encourage the children to give their piece of pottery to a friend, who can then try to complete the picture of the galley based on the 'evidence' they have.

3. Pirates!

Age range
Seven to eleven.

Group size
Pairs.

What you need
Reference books on pirates, ships and seafarers.

What to do
Pirates are often seen as colourful and exciting figures around whom a certain mythology has grown up. Ask the children to write down a list of everything they know about pirates. This might include such things as the names of famous pirates and pirate ships, the pirate hat, how, when and where they attacked other ships and so on. They could also include in their lists any cartoon or comic pirates they know. How did the children learn so much about pirates? This activity will demonstrate how far an understanding of the past can be coloured by popular myths. Ask the children to find out from the reference books how much of what they know can be substantiated by evidence. Can they also find some other things they did not know about pirates?

Further activity
Ask the children to research in more detail a specific element of the topic such as how pirates boarded a ship, or what they did if they captured a ship or what happened to them when they were caught.

4. Ships' food

Age range
Seven to eleven.

Group size
Pairs.

What you need
Items of fresh food such as fruit, meat and biscuits; preservatives such as salt, water, boxes, a dark room.

What to do
Sailing for long periods of time led to a major problem concerned with keeping food fresh. Ask the children to devise and monitor an experiment to see how long different kinds of food would stay fresh if locked away in boxes in dark rooms. They could also compare what would happen to similar kinds of food if it were left out in daylight and fresh air. Tell the children to check the food for a week and record what has happened. Why do some foods stay fresh longer than others?

Ask the children to investigate what measures sailors took to preserve their foods. They could then repeat their experiments, this time having covered the meat in salt or pickled vegetables. The children will then be able to compare the results of their two experiments.

Further activity
Ask the children to think about the practical problems of food going off on board ship such as diseases like scurvy. What methods of preservation are used today to keep food fresher for longer?

5. The press-gang

Age range
Nine to eleven.

Group size
Small groups or the whole class.

What you need
Reference books about ships and shipping in the eighteenth and nineteenth centuries (only needed if the children are to do the background work for themselves), a large hall.

What to do

Life for sailors in the eighteenth and nineteenth centuries was very harsh: It often began with able-bodied men being 'press-ganged' or forced into service, usually after being encouraged to drink too much in coastal taverns!

Explain this to the children and ask them to dramatise a press ganging.
• What characteristics in a person would the press-gang be looking for?
• How would they go about their business?
• What would the reaction be of the men they met?
• At what moment would the press-gang strike?
• What would the reaction be of the men who had been press-ganged once they realised what had happened to them?

Let each group dramatise their own press-ganging and perform to the rest of the class. The children can then choose which drama looks the most realistic.

Further activities

Teach the children some sea shanties and other songs which were popular amongst sailors of the time. They could also write a story about how one young man was press-ganged into the navy following a drunken evening in Portsmouth!

6. A ship's and sailor's dictionary

Age range

Nine to eleven.

Group size

Individuals.

What you need

Dictionaries, reference books about ships and shipping.

What to do

Listed below are a number of words associated with ships and shipping through history. Ask the children to find out what these words mean:
• aftercastle – the fighting platform at the rear of medieval ships;
• boom – wooden pole along bottom of sail;
• broadside – all guns on one side of a ship firing at once;
• caulking – plugging the holes between wooden planks with tarred rope for water proofing;
• cross-staff – wooden instrument used to find latitude in navigation;
• fathom – distance of 1.8m (6ft) used to measure the depth of water;
• galley – kitchen area of a ship, also a type of rowed boat;
• grog – mixture of water and rum drunk by sailors;
• jib – triangular sail rigged in front of the mast;
• periscope – tube with mirrors used on submarines to see above water line while submerged;
• sextant – navigational instrument used to calculate a ship's position;
• tiller – the handle which controls the rudder.

Additionally, the children can try to date, approximately, to which period in the history of ships and shipping each word is most relevant. They can then also draw a diagram of the item concerned.

Further activity

Can the children find any nautical terminology which was first used in the twentieth century? Conversely, can they find terminology still in use today from, say, five hundred or more years ago?

BACKGROUND

Food and farming

As eating is a basic human need, people have always had to find ways of feeding themselves. Early humans would have begun by hunting animals and gathering food such as nuts, berries, fruit and seeds. Survival depended on a constant hunt for food and entailed people continually moving around from place to place. Eventually, however, from about 700BC onwards, people realised that they could sow seeds and tame animals which meant that they were able to stay in one place, living and working in groups as farmers. Herding and grain harvesting probably first began in the Middle East, but by 3500BC, Europe including

Britain, was farming as well. During the Neolithic period, men and women began to use ploughs and to develop a range of other tools and implements which were made from flint and pottery.

The development of city states and empires coupled with technical developments such as fermentation and the selective cultivation of cereals meant that food production became increasingly sophisticated. Additionally, technical advancement in the manufacturing of pottery and metals assisted in food production as foods were able to be baked and cooked quickly and efficiently. States such as Greece and Rome had

patterns of social organisation that regularised food production with certain groups of people whose job it was to work on the land and produce food. It was also at this time that religion began to influence the production of food with certain gods being thought to govern farming, the weather and food and drink.

The Romans in Britain, particularly after the birth of Christ, were extremely sophisticated as farmers and preparers of food. Tools and equipment were readily available and cooks were able to benefit from a division of

labour which had specific people who were allowed to do tasks such as producing bread, wine and meat. Importantly too, at this time, the idea of having a meal as an important social occasion began to develop, with a three course main meal being eaten in the evening.

By the time the Celts came to Britain in AD500, they were already well-known as farmers and husbanders. It was the Celts who developed the idea of salting meat for preservation and the Celtic home was built around the hearth. Celtic kitchen equipment included such things as pails, dishes, griddles and, most importantly, a cauldron in which the main meals such as broths and stews could be cooked.

The information we have about the Anglo-Saxons tends to be derived from books written by monks and according to these sources peasant food changed very little from this time right the way through until the fifteenth century. These sources have to be treated with caution in that the monks would not necessarily have known all the details of what peasants would have eaten. The monks themselves who wrote these accounts would have eaten reasonably well or would have mixed with those that did. It was largely based on butter, milk, cheese, eggs, bacon and porridge. All of these would be generated by families from the products of their small amounts of livestock. Any surplus that was produced would be used to pay their dues to the lord or church or buy cooking items or utensils.

After the Norman conquest, the control of the land through the feudal system became more developed. The king would let out part of his land to his barons in return for their support. This system was continued downwards through society – through knights, villeins and serfs. In addition, there also existed a group of farmers who only had small holdings and were known as yeoman. These farmers owed their allegiance directly to the king.

Whereas the food for peasants and serfs remained much the same throughout the Middle Ages, a very different standard existed for royalty, nobles and churchmen. Recipes were used from all over Europe and banquets and feasts became important social occasions.

By the Tudor and Stuart times, land was no longer the only source of income. Although land was still important, money was also generated through commerce and trade. The Tudors however, continued to build great halls in their houses in which the kitchen had an important central place. New food and drink became available too, about this time, as explorers returned from foreign lands with exotic spices, fruits and vegetables.

The eigtheenth and nineteenth centuries were times of rapid change in farming. In the eighteenth century, farmers became interested in developing root crops which would feed their animals all the year round. This meant that they were able to increase the amounts of livestock that their land could support. However, many peasants who had traditionally owned small strips of land and a cow and a sheep lost out in that their land was then used for the grazing of livestock and life became very hard for country people.

The nineteenth century saw a number of bad harvests which brought immense misery. The 1840s and 1850s saw periods of particular difficulty. It was also a time of industrialisation which meant that there was better transport for food, the development of new methods of cooking such as stoves and new ways of storing food in cans.

The twentieth century has seen the continual reduction of the number of people who work on the land. However, food production, distribution and sales are now, collectively, one of the major areas of British industry.

It is difficult to highlight specific dates in the history of food and farming as changes were only discernible over very long periods of time.

Teaching plan

A series of lessons and activities on food and farming could be organised as follows.
• Food and farming before the birth of Christ.
• The Feudal System.
• How technological change has affected food and farming over time.
• Food from animals, fish and birds.
• Recipes from different periods of history.
• Food and health through time.
• The farming year.

Links could also be made with each of the core study units as the children explore all aspects of each of these periods in history.

ACTIVITIES

1. Farming and food rhymes

Age range
Seven to nine.

Group size
Individuals or pairs.

What you need
Photocopiable page 184, poetry or rhyme books.

What to do
Photocopiable page 184 shows a number of old short rhymes associated with food and farming. A brief description has been given of the origins of the rhyme, although the children may well need to think further about what the rhyme refers to. Ask the children to learn these rhymes off by heart. They could then use poetry books to see whether they can find any other poems that refer to food. Can they suggest what the origins of these additional rhymes might be?

The children could then present their rhymes to a wider audience, such as at a school assembly. Perhaps other children in the school might suggest ideas as to what the origins of these rhymes might be?

Further activity
Poems and rhymes are often an interesting way of investigating the past. Look at other well-known, traditional rhymes and explain their background to the children. Can they write their own poems and make up their own rhymes about twentieth-century food, for example cooking using a microwave or eating a hamburger in a fast food restaurant?

2. Pot luck

Age range
Seven to eleven.

Group size
Pairs.

What you need
Pot Luck: Cooking and recipes from the past by Jo Lawrie (A & C Black, 1991).

What to do
The book, *Pot Luck*, provides a collection of recipes from the past and includes recipes from all the periods covered in the core study units, except Ancient Greece. If you are doing a 'Food and farming' topic, select a recipe from each of the periods covered in the book and ask pairs of children to provide the ingredients and prepare the dish. Invite other classes, parents, governors and so on to a 'food-from-the-past' tasting session in which the children can describe which ingredients they used to prepare the recipes and which methods were used.

The children could also illustrate the session by providing drawings and paintings of the food and farming methods used in the period concerned. Better still, the children can dress up in costumes appropriate to the period and serve the food in the appropriate manner; for example, a Victorian dish could be served at a table with a formal setting.

Further activity
Ask the children to bring in recipes which have been handed down through their families. How far back do they go?

3. A disastrous year

Age range
Eight to eleven.

Group size
Individuals.

What you need
Extract from *Anglo-Saxon Chronicles*, reference books on Anglo-Saxon farming.

What to do
Throughout history, farming has been a problematic process, as many things can go wrong. In 1103, the following happened in the Peterborough area:

'It was a very disastrous year here in this country by reason of numerous taxes and also as a result of murrain and the ruin of the harvest, both of the corn and of the fruit on all the trees.

Further, the wind did such great damage here in the land to all the crops that nobody remembered anything like it before.'

This extract could be used in two ways. You might like to use it as a starting point for imaginative and creative writing as the children write about what it would have been like to be a farmer in such a year. Alternatively, you might like to use it as a source of further research, asking the children such questions as:

• What taxes were imposed in 1103 and why, in general, would new taxes need to be raised?
• What is 'murrain'?
• What sort of things could have caused the ruin of the corn and fruit?

Further activity
Ask the children to investigate other periods in time when food and farming were affected by natural or man-made problems, such as the nineteenth-century potato famines or the effect of the Second World War on food supplies.

4. Family food

Age range
Eight to eleven.

Group size
Individuals.

What you need
No special requirements.

What to do
This activity allows children to investigate the memories of their own families, particularly their parents and grandparents. It will help the children to realise that there have been significant changes in eating patterns even over the past 20 or 30 years. Ask them to devise some questions to put to their relatives; for example:
• What things would you have typically eaten at breakfast, lunch and dinner?
• What products that you ate when you were young are still on the market today? What changes have you noticed in they way they are packaged and sold?
• What non-British food did you eat when you were young?
• What were your favourite drinks?
• Are there any foods which you ate when you were young which are no longer available?
• Did you ever eat out at restaurants?

Encourage the children to analyse the data they collect. Tell them to:
• look out for things which are different and things have remained the same;
• find out if people eat out more today than 20 or 30 years ago;
• see whether there is a greater selection of foods available today than there used to be.

Further activity

Ask the children to prepare a book entitled 'Food: yesterday and today' in which they compare their views about food with their families' recollections from the past. They could also look at how technological advances have changed patterns of food and farming.

5. Hunting for food

Age range
Nine to eleven.

Group size
Small groups of four or less.

What you need
Wood, paper, card, stones, adhesive, string.

What to do
Introduce the children to some of the simple implements used by ancient hunters and then set them the task of preparing a replica of an implement which they think could have been used to hunt for animals. Although they will be allowed to use modern materials, restrict the number so that they begin to understand the limited resources which ancient hunters would have had.

When they have done this, ask the children to describe how they would go about hunting animals in their small group. How would they ensnare a wild boar or catch a fish?

Further activity
Ancient hunters developed farming techniques because they discovered that they could grow crops from seeds. Give the children a variety of seeds and ask them to plant them and observe them as they grow.

6. A food time-line

Age range
Nine to eleven.

Group size
Individuals.

What you need
Pictures of various foods, reference books on food.

What to do
List a number of well-known foods and ask the children to investigate when they were first introduced into this country and where they came from. They could then make a time-line identifying the different periods in which various foods were introduced.

Ask the children to investigate why the sixteenth and twentieth centuries saw the introduction of more new foods into this country than any other periods.

Further activity
The children could identify where foodstuffs have come from on a world map. They could also use the reference books to investigate which foods have been exported from Britain over time.

Houses and places of worship

Shelter is a basic human need and therefore, the first 'homes' would probably have been just that, for example under trees or in caves. There was little need for permanence as ancient peoples were nomadic, moving from place to place in search of food. However, as farming began to develop and communities stayed longer in the same place, more sophisticated shelters were made by building frames of branches and covering them with woven reeds, clay or skins.

During the Bronze and Iron ages, when tribes were at war, homes were built on lakes or marshes as these areas provided better defence against attack. Attackers could be seen when they were still some distance away and houses were built off the ground on stilts to make them harder to attack. Over time people began to build houses, usually wattle and daub thatched huts, in groups forming settlements or encampments.

The architecture of the Romans changed all this; their houses were made of stone and incorporated a variety of rooms within one building, including, in the largest houses, a chapel for the worship of the household gods. They also built sophisticated heating systems and used materials which were more difficult to work with, such as marble. The most important officials built country houses, surrounded by a wider estate. When the Romans left, it was to be almost 1000 years before such grand houses were again seen in Britain.

The Anglo-Saxons reverted back to building simple wattle and daub structures, based on wooden frames, even for a Saxon Chief. They did not bother very much about decorating these dwellings and the centre piece was a huge stone hearth. Poorer people however, continued to use wattle and daub for building their huts. The exceptions to this were Saxon churches which had more elaborate architecture and decoration.

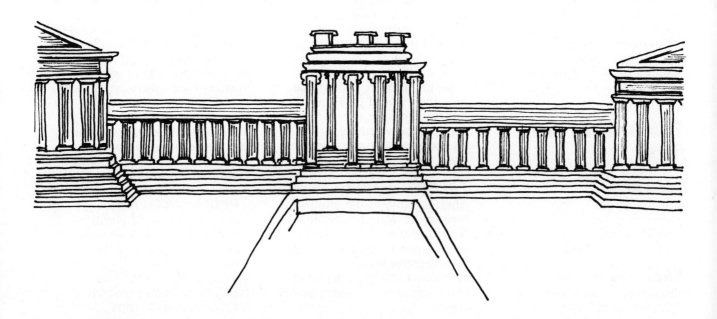

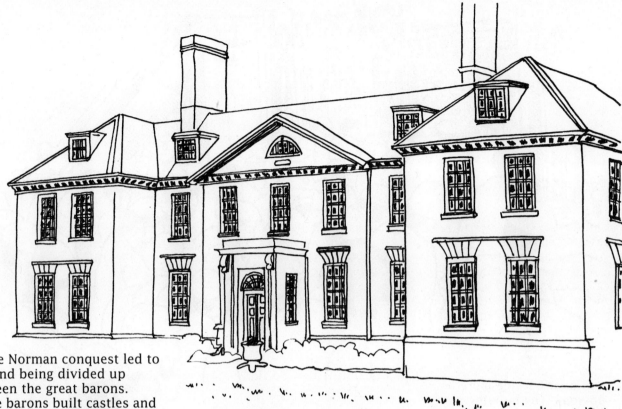

The Norman conquest led to England being divided up between the great barons. These barons built castles and manor houses, but again, internally, these were quite simple the main feature being a large hall. As well as building large dwellings this was also the period when many of the cathedrals were started and built. This was as a consequence of the kings of England taking religion increasingly seriously.

By the later Middle Ages houses had become more sophisticated again. Building styles changed with arches becoming pointed and windows being made larger. Although the large houses were still built around a central hall, improvements were made such as adding on a musicians gallery, hanging tapestries on the wall and furnishing rooms with carved furniture. In many cases, there would also be a chapel, kitchen and many bedrooms. During this time and through the Tudor and Stuart period,

town houses too became more popular. These houses tended to be built fairly close together and the streets were extremely narrow. The rooms had low ceilings and the ground floor was dug below street level. Houses also began to have more elegant exteriors and the Tudor period is perhaps best remembered for the magnificent houses built by the rich. They used bricks and slate, and tiles began to replace thatch as roofing material. Also during this period, the conditions in which the poorer people lived began to improve. Small cottages were built, often with a brick chimney.

The Stuart period was a time of increasing influences from abroad. Inigo Jones introduced the craft of being an architect and designing homes for other people, particularly royalty.

The Georgian period was a period of immense wealth and which was mostly obtained through trade. This period is often thought of as the golden age of house building with huge country houses being designed and built. Many of these homes were built in 'classical' style with pillared fronts. Architects such as Robert Adam and William Kent were renouned for both their interior and exterior designs. This period also saw the development of immense gardens. However, in contrast there were ever increasing numbers of poor people who were forced to live in appalling conditions in the towns.

During the nineteenth century the differences between the houses of the rich

and poor became more obvious. The building of factories in particular localities meant that an industrial workforce had to be housed nearby. This led to the growth of districts of small courts and narrow alleys and small houses. Such properties were dark and overcrowded with little or no sanitation.

Places of worship became less grand over the later centuries as popular religion grew. The Medieval cathedrals still dominated religious architecture, but simple chapels and churches grew up over the country in the seventeenth, eighteenth and nineteenth centuries, as poorer people were evangelised by men like John Wesley. In the twentieth century numerous different types of places of worship became increasingly common as Britain has become multicultural with Mosques, temples and synagogues found in most cities.

The twentieth century has also seen a huge range of new housing styles emerge with the increasing wealth of the majority of the population. Suburbs and large out-of-town housing estates grew up around large towns and cities and new towns were also created. In the 1950s and 1960s, high-rise flats were designed as a solution to homelessness and overcrowded housing conditions; but they brought with them a whole range of other social problems and even today, with the housing conditions for the majority of the population better than they have ever been, there are still problems of quality and quantity.

It is difficult to highlight specific dates in the history of houses and places of worship as changes in style took place over a long period of time and were very largely incremental.

Teaching plan

A series of lessons and activities on 'Houses and places of worship' could be organised as follows.
• The first houses and homes of ancient man.
• A Roman household.
• Cathedrals.
• The construction of houses and homes through history.
• House styles.
• Inside a place of worship.
• In service.

Links could also be made with core study units 1 to 5, as well as the supplementary study unit 'Domestic life', 'families and childhood' and those looking at studies of a past non-European societies.

ACTIVITIES

1. Stained-glass windows

Age range
Seven to eleven.

Group size
Individuals.

What you need
Black sugar paper, scissors, coloured tissue paper, photocopiable page 185.

What to do
As part of more specific work on cathedrals, the children can look, in particular, at stained-glass windows.

Begin by asking the children why they think the stone masons built such huge windows into the cathedrals. Look at the process of making a stained-glass window and study examples of the kinds of images and stories which appear on them. Ask the children to choose an appropriate theme and design their own stained-glass window. Let them explore the light patterns made by cutting out black sugar paper into the shape of a cathedral window frame. They can then stick different coloured pieces of tissue paper on to the back of the frame and put their designs up on the windows, so that the light shines through them. The children could also design their own patterns for a stained glass window using photocopiable page 185. It could either have one large image on it, such as a saint, or be made up of a number of smaller images depicting, for example, a story from the Bible.

Further activity
Can the children find any examples of stained-glass windows in local churches? What stories if any do the stained glass windows tell? How long have they been there?

2. A home in history

Age range
Eight to eleven.

Group size
The whole class.

What you need
Camera, sketch pads, pencils, local history books.

What to do
Every school, no matter where it is situated, will have easy access to an historical home – even if this is only a house of one year old! Take the children to visit a house, if possible so that they can look at it both internally and externally. They should pretend to be historical detectives looking for clues about the age of the house. In advance of the visit, ask the children what they should be looking for. This might include:
• the shape and structure of the building;
• visible signs of age such as the building discolouring;
• evidence of dates such as those carved in the stonework or brickwork;
• internal evidence, for example kitchenettes.
   Ask the children to sketch different features of the building and take photographs of what they consider to be the key piece of evidence. It is also helpful if they are able to talk to the present occupants of the house or examine records and documents relevant to the house. How far back can they trace the history of the house?

Further activity
Although there is more 'obvious' history in an older house, it is worth using a more modern house which is still occupied. The children can interview the occupants of the house and ask them to describe their memories of the house. Is there any way of tracing previous occupants of the house and asking them for their memories? This is an exercise the children can repeat for themselves in their own homes.

3. A house time-line

Age range
Nine to eleven.

Group size
Pairs.

What you need
Reference books on the history of houses and homes.

What to do
Children are likely to already have there own impressions of houses and homes through time, formed by their general knowledge and what they have read or seen. Therefore, begin by asking pairs of children to sketch pictures of houses, homes and other buildings from any period of history. Ask them to note down

anything they know, in particular, about any building. They should then use reference books to research in more detail the houses they have drawn. They could add a time-line to their pictures showing how the particular type of building they have concentrated on has changed over time.

Ask them to look critically at the houses and homes shown in the reference books. Do they reflect adequately the living conditions of people from different sections of society or do they concentrate on the houses of well-off or rich people? Ask the children why they think this might be the case.

Further activity
Ask the children to look at two

periods of housing styles in depth, for example the Tudor and Stuart and Victorian times, and see what similarities and differences they can find between the buildings that were built in these periods.

4. Cathedral map of Britain

Age range
Nine to eleven.

Group size
Individuals.

What you need
Photocopiable page 186, atlas, reference books on cathedrals and places of worship.

What to do
Photocopiable page 186 provides an outline map of Britain together with a list of some of the most famous

cathedral towns in the country. Ask the children to use the atlas to find where on the map each cathedral can be located and mark them on to the photocopiable page by drawing a cathedral symbol. In addition, they should find out why and when when the cathedrals were built. The children might also discover that some places such as Londonderry have more than one cathedral and other places such as Coventry have cathedrals which have been virtually rebuilt.

The children could then look at two or three of the cathedrals in detail and see if they can find out more about them – for example, any famous events which took place in the cathedrals or famous bishops and archbishops.

Further activity
Ask the children to design a modern cathedral which includes the main elements of a traditional cathedral, but in a more modern style.

5. Slum!

Age range
Nine to eleven.

Group size
Individuals.

What you need
Reference books on houses and homes in the early twentieth century.

What to do
It is important in a topic on 'Houses and places of worship' not to forget that the living conditions of vast sections of the population have been, through time and are still today, extremely poor. Ask the children to research the housing conditions of very poor people at the beginning of the century. They could look at sanitation, overcrowding, dampness and the consequences of all these problems for the people who lived in such houses. They should then imagine that they are public health inspectors, who had gone to see the conditions for themselves, and write a report about the conditions they have seen. They could also imagine that they are MPs in and around 1900 and prepare speeches on housing conditions and make proposals to improve them.

Further activity
Although this needs to be handled with considerable sensitivity, the children could compare the poorest housing conditions of today with the poorest conditions at the turn of the century. Have there been improvements? Are these of any relevance if you are stuck in poor housing conditions today?

BACKGROUND

Writing and printing

The first forms of known written communication were the drawings of Early Man which recorded such exploits as hunting and fighting. These drawings were scratched on to tree bark or stone or painted on the walls of a cave using dyes. This method of pictorial communication continued for a long time. The Ancient Egyptians used a script which was based on drawings and scratched on to clay tablets. These pictures gradually evolved into shapes which, over time, came to represent particular sounds. In parallel to this, the Sumerians of Mesopotamia were also developing a script (known as *cuneiform*) which was used to represent words and syllables. They would use the end of a reed, cut into a wedge shape, to press into soft clay to make this writing.

The Egyptians also invented a new writing material called papyrus, made from the papyrus reed. This was lighter and easier to work with than clay and could be written on using a simple reed pen. At the same time that papyrus was being developed (pre-3500BC), parchment was also being invented in Egypt. Parchment was made from animal skins which were stretched, scraped and polished.

Progressively, as the actual mechanics of writing became easier, so the script became simpler with pictures evolving into letters. The Phoenicians, a Mediterranean trading people, introduced a simple writing script to Europe. This was adopted and adapted by both the Greeks and the Romans and from it grew the notion that letters of the alphabet (from the first two letters of the Greek alphabet *alpha* and *beta*) could be grouped together to make all the words in the language.

The presentation of writing was further developed by the Romans who used a pointed instrument known as a *stylus* with which to write. In addition, they attached wooden rollers to the end of sheets of parchment and made scrolls.

The first real books and the encouragement of people devoted to study and writing arose from the church. Monks wrote down parts of the Bible and recorded other events and happenings. They also prepared, illustrated or illuminated other manuscripts and these they sewed together to create books.

The development of this work was assisted by the invention of paper. Paper-making was probably first developed by the Chinese in AD100. The Chinese are also credited with the invention of printing, sometime near the end of the sixth century.

By the middle of the fifteenth century, trading and education had spread the knowledge of books beyond those associated with the church. This was helped by the most significant development of all, the invention of printing by movable type. Essentially, this involved individual letters, which were made of metal, being used to print multiple copies of a text. Importantly, these metal letters could be used time after time. This invention was made by a German mirror-maker called Johann Gutenberg, who used this method for the first time to produce a copy of the Bible.

Initially, Gutenberg, and Caxton working in England, sought to imitate handwriting. However, books slowly began to be printed using simpler forms of type and in languages other than Latin.

The next major development in the spread of writing, printing and literacy was the appearance at the beginning of the sixteenth century of newspapers. The first newspapers were just single page leaflets, produced weekly, but over time larger pages were used. The first daily newsheet was the *Daily Courant* which was published in 1702. In 1785, *The Times* was produced for the first time although for the first three years of its life it was known as *The Daily Universal Register*.

Not surprisingly, the industrial revolution brought about new developments in the printing process. The first power-operated printing press was used in 1811 and was driven by a steam engine.

The most dramatic changes occurred however, in the twentieth century. Education for the masses led to an increase in literacy across the whole population and improvements in communication and increasing

democracy meant that there was an almost insatiable demand for information. In more recent years, with the development of computer technology, printing and writing has become quicker and easier with many people using desk top publishing systems and machines. In addition, written communication plays a major part in modern society through advertising, magazines, books and newspapers.

Key dates

c.30,000BC: *Homo sapiens* first produced cave paintings and sculptures.
c.3,500BC: the Sumerian civilisation developed *cuneiform* writing.

c.3,000BC: pictorial writing in Ancient Egypt.
c.900BC: probably the date when Homer wrote his epics.
c.AD100: Invention of paper by the Chinese.
500–1500: Writing and printing was largely in the hands of the Church and, in particular, the monks.
c.594: Invention of printing by the Chinese.
1440–1450: Invention of printing with movable type by Johann Gutenberg.
1476: William Caxton set up his printing press in Westminster.
c.1500: Appearance of the first newspapers in Britain.
1702: first daily newspaper.
1712: newspaper tax introduced in England.
1785: *The Daily Universal Register* began and became *The Times* three years later.
1811: Invention of steam power operated press by Walter Koenig.

1890: first typesetting machine, called Linotype, invented.
Twentieth century: Mass communication and publication of a variety of printed media.

Teaching plan

A series of lessons and activities on writing and printing could be organised as follows.
• Writing and printing before the time of Christ.
• The role of the Church through the ages in promoting literacy.
• Gutenberg and Caxton.
• The history of newspapers.
• Education, writing and printing.
• Forms of writing and scripts through time.
• Written communication in the twentieth century.
   Links could also be made with core study units 2 to 6. In addition, it may be worth looking at supplementary study units 'Houses and places of worship', 'Domestic life, Families and childhood', 'Ancient Egypt' and 'Mesopotamia'.

ACTIVITIES

1. Seals

Age range
Seven to nine.

Group size
Individuals.

What you need
'Block' printing materials, for example, polystyrene, ink, wax.

What to do
Throughout history seals have played an important part in the 'control' of printed work. From Babylon through Ancient Egypt to medieval Europe and beyond they have indicated the mark of government. Ask the children to investigate seals and, in particular, to try and find examples of where seals are still used today, for example at, the post office, solicitors and so on.

The children could then make up their own seals from a polystyrene block, cutting out the correct shape and printing with it using printing inks. Alternatively, with assistance, they could use melted wax and shape it accordingly on a mock historical document they have written. Can the children design a seal for their own family?

Further activity
Ask the children to examine the ways in which documents today are made 'official'. Ask them to look at forms, legal stationery, signatures and so on. Why do there need to be controls on the written and printed word?

2. A writing emporium

Age range
Seven to eleven.

Group size
Individuals, small groups, the whole class or several classes in the school.

What you need
A variety of materials to allow children to write using methods from different periods of history such as clay, sticks, mud, sand, goose feathers, slate boards and so on.

What to do

In order to give children an understanding of how people wrote in different periods of history, set up a writing emporium in the school hall. Organise a variety of different activities to allow the children to experience, at first hand, different methods of writing and printing. These could include:
• engraving on a wax or clay tablet;
• using a stick and dried mud on stiff card (or brown paint) to make a cave painting;
• using a goose feather quill with ink;
• writing on a slate board with a slate pencil;
• printing by various techniques such as press printing (potato or block printing) and linocut printing;
• making paper;

• writing and printing using computer graphics.

The school hall could be arranged as a giant time-line so that the children can progress through the different developmental stages of writing and printing. In the classroom, the children could make their own collection of ancient and modern writing implements and try writing with each of these in turn.

Further activity

This 'writing emporium' and work on the history of writing and printing could be done as part of a wider school-based project on a 'Pen to Paper' theme concerning anything to do with written communication in which children write letters, stories, poems, scripts, holiday postcards and so on. They could also look at different forms of writing such as hymn writing, writing for newspapers, illustrating books and magazines and the teaching of writing. Each of these, in their own way, could

be given an historical dimension; for example the children could look at and practise the different kinds of handwriting styles that have been taught to children over the past hundred years or so.

3. Censored!

Age range
Nine to eleven.

Group size
Individuals, small groups or the whole class.

What you need
No special requirements.

What to do
The written and printed word has always been a powerful source of dissent. Begin a class discussion by asking the children to list reasons why they think some books might be banned. Ask them what they think about the effects of such bans and who imposes bans. You could then describe different periods in British and world history when materials have been banned, for example the Reformation or Nazi Germany.

Divide the children into two groups to prepare arguments for and against the motion, 'There are no circumstances in which books should be banned'. Ask two or three children from both sides to prepare their group's case which they can present to the rest of the class. The discussion can be concluded by asking children to vote and express their own views on the subject.

Further activity
Ask the children to look at newspapers from one week and see if they can find examples of books or other materials that have been banned. What reasons have been given for banning them?

What counter arguments could be given? What do the children themselves think?

4. A history of advertising

Age range
Nine to eleven.

Group size
Individuals and small groups.

What you need
Reference books on the history of advertising, old advertising posters, advertisements from newspapers.

What to do
No study of writing and printing would be complete without an analysis of advertising, which has exploited writing in a variety of ways and forms, for example with catchy slogans.

Ask the children to consider why people advertise and what advertising there was in the past before formal writing and printing. The children could begin by looking at street advertising in Rome. They could then look at pictorial signs from the medieval period, when a non-literate public would recognise the sign of a large pair of scissors as indicating a tailor, and a tankard for an alehouse.

Tell the children to consider the role of newspapers in advertising. Ask them to look at copies of old newspapers and compare the adverts in them with the adverts in newspapers today. Is there less writing in current adverts than in the past? Why do the children think this is? Could it be because techniques are more sophisticated?

When the children study advertising in the twentieth century, they should look at the messages which print has

conveyed. In particular, they could look at advertising slogans, such as 'Go to work on an egg', and could examine the role of women in advertisements. Finally, they could look at some adverts which are so sophisticated that they don't use print at all, but are still easily identifiable as advertisements for particular products.

Further activity
A topic on 'Advertising' offers excellent opportunities for studying the role of communication over time. The children can look at how a message is communicated, what means are used and how people respond to these messages. In particular, they

could consider the influence mass literacy has had in enabling people to have access to information about goods, products and services.

5. An illuminated manuscript

Age range
Ten to eleven.

Group size
Individuals.

What you need
Photocopiable page 187, ink pens, reference books about writing and printing.

What to do
Photocopiable page 187 provides an example of an illuminated manuscript. The children could copy the letters given in the example and write

their own sentence in an illuminated style. Ask them to examine the contexts of this type of manuscript. They could investigate questions such as:
• Who wrote such manuscripts?
• What was the purpose of the illumination?
• Who would read such manuscripts?
• What would the content of such manuscripts be?
    The children could use the background information to provide their own text, for example a passage from the Bible. On the third part of the photocopiable sheet, the children could use a modern script and method of printing (such as a word processor) to provide the same text.

Further activity
Gather together the photocopiable sheets from all the children in the class and bind them together to make a book of manuscripts.

BACKGROUND

Land transport

Early humans had to travel around on foot. Gradually, animals such as donkeys, camels and horses were trained so that they would carry people and equipment. However, the most significant development in terms of transport, was the development of the wheel. It is generally believed that the Sumerian people of Mesopotamia invented the wheel sometime between 3,000 and 4,000BC. These first wheels were made from solid wood and fixed to a thick piece of wood which acted as an axle. Archeological evidence indicates that wheels were first used in Britain at around the same time as in Mesopotamia and certainly, by the time the Roman forces invaded Britain, wheel technology was quite sophisticated with the Britons using chariots to fight against the invaders.

The societies of Ancient Greece and Rome had also made use of wheel technology. The Romans, in particular, had seen the importance of building roads in order to improve communication and facilitate the movement of armies to different parts of a conquered kingdom. Their road building technology was excellent and they knew about bridge building which also improved the speed of transport across the land. Different kinds of wheeled vehicles evolved from the initial two-wheeled cart which was used to transport important Roman people. For example, four-wheeled wagons were used by farmers to transport heavy loads.

Even after the Romans had left Britain and other parts of Europe, the legacy of their roads remained. In fact, these roads were built so well that they took many years to decay. But, inevitably, they fell into disrepair, particularly because the Saxons were unable to make the good quality cement needed to maintain them.

To a large extent, transport developments stood still for many hundreds of years after the decline of the Roman empire. When a large item, such as stone for new buildings, was needed, if it was not found locally, then it was transported by water

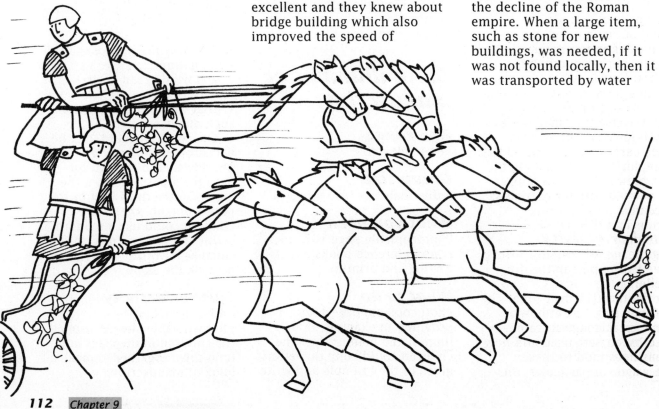

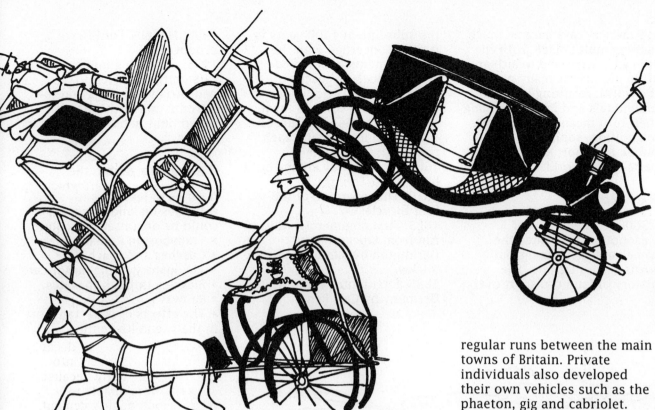

where possible. Trade was carried out using pack horses which transported items from one part of the country to another. However, with the Normans came a commitment to maintain the highways. They began to collect tolls on important roads and this money assisted the building and repairing of roads. The roads themselves were filled with many travellers, including merchants, lawyers and pilgrims and this led to, in addition, inns being built along these routes to offer a place of rest to weary travellers.

By the time the Tudor Kings and Queens came to the throne, carriages and coaches, pulled by horses, were increasingly popular. The stage-wagon by this time, was

a common sight. This was a huge wagon, pulled by eight or ten horses. It could only travel short distances at any stretch, but it marked the beginning of a regular transport service for both goods and passengers.

During the seventeenth century, coach technology improved with springs being used for the first time and the first glass windows were fitted into a coach made for James, Duke of York. The roads were still quite poor and the traveller had to put up with many discomforts, not least, the marauding bands of highwaymen and robbers.

The eighteenth century saw a gradual recognition that new roads had to be built. Engineers such as John Metcalfe, Thomas Telford and John Macadam made significant advances in road building. This helped the development of the stage-coach service which made

regular runs between the main towns of Britain. Private individuals also developed their own vehicles such as the phaeton, gig and cabriolet.

As towns developed during the nineteenth century there was a huge increase in the number of coaches on the road and roadside inns became major centres. Yet, land transport was to change forever with the coming of industrialisation. In particular, the railways almost single-handedly destroyed the coaching industry even though attempts were made to apply steam technology to road vehicles. The nineteenth century also saw the invention of the bicycle and today's bicycle is virtually the same as the safety bicycle of the late 1880s.

However, it was the coming of the internal combustion engine that land transport revolutionised. It was a German, Carl Benz, who built the first motor car in 1885, but up until the First World War, motoring was an expensive pastime. After the war, and largely due to mass production in America, cars became much more commonplace. With the car came increased wealth and affluence across many parts of the world, resulting in private individuals and families having their own means of transport. In addition, sophisticated public transport exists in many parts of the world.

Key dates

*c.*3000BC: Sumerians of Mesopotamia invented the wheel and the Romans built roads across Europe. The history of land transport over the subsequent 1500 years is largely concerned with the improvements of wheeled vehicles such as coaches.
*c.*1657: First passenger service by coach from town to town.
1663: Toll gates introduced.
1784: First Royal Mail coach from Bath to London.
1804: First railway engine built by Richard Trevithick.
1810: The invention of the first bicycle.
1825: First commercial railway run from Stockton to Darlington by Stephenson's *Rocket*.
1885: First motor car built in Germany by Carl Benz.
1908: Model T Ford first produced.
1935: Increasing numbers of cars on the road led to pedestrian crossings and the introduction of the 30 mph speed limit in built up areas in Britain.

Teaching plan

A series of lessons and activities on land transport could be organised as follows.
• Transport in Roman times.
• Coaches and coaching.
• The history of the motor car.
• Bicycles through the ages.
• Railways.
• The effects of land transport in the twentieth century.

ACTIVITIES

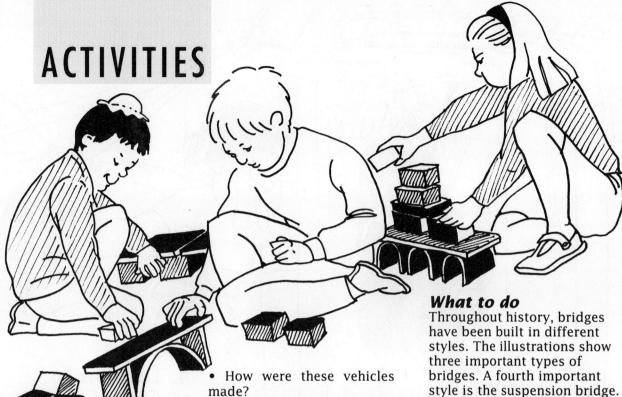

1. Roman transport

Age range
Seven to nine.

Group size
Individuals or pairs.

What you need
Reference books on Roman times or transport, wood (including wheel shapes), cardboard, simple tools, fabric scraps.

What to do
Begin by asking the children to find out as much as they can about the different kinds of transport used in Roman times. This could include chariots, litters and wagons. Ask them to find out various things about these kinds of transport:

• How were these vehicles made?
• Who would have used them?
• What were their advantages and disadvantages?
    Set the children the task of making *working* models of each of the items. They could then decorate and paint them as appropriate.

Further activity
The children could choose two or three other periods in history and make similar models. Can they create, for example, the effect of using springs in their models?

2. Bridges

Age range
Seven to eleven.

Group size
Pairs.

What you need
Card, scissors, other 'junk' material, adhesive, reference books.

What to do
Throughout history, bridges have been built in different styles. The illustrations show three important types of bridges. A fourth important style is the suspension bridge. Ask the children to see what they can find out about each of the styles:
• What is the earliest reference they can find about such a bridge?
• What materials has the bridge been made from?
• Can they find the names of famous engineers who have built such bridges?
• Are there examples of such bridges in the locality?
• Can they put the locations of such bridges on a map of Britain?
    Then ask the children to build their own bridges in each of the styles. Can they devise a test to find out how strong each bridge is?

Further activity
Ask the children to research the bridges in the local area. When were they built? For what purpose have they been built? Who opened them? Are there any famous stories or characters associated with the bridges?

3. The first train

Age range
Seven to eleven.

Group size
Individuals.

What you need
Reference books relating to early railways.

What to do
Given that they live in a technological world, children find it hard to comprehend what it must have been like when machines like trains first appeared. Ask them to research the background to Stephenson's *Rocket*. They could imagine that they are newspaper reporters who have been sent to cover the story of the *Rocket's* first run. Essentially, they need to describe everything they see as if they have never seen it before. They could describe such things as how the *Rocket* was powered, what shape it was, how it stayed on the rails and so on. The children could write the report in a sceptical tone as if they believed that the whole enterprise was doomed to failure!

Further activity
Can the children find reports from other people of the same period? How did they view the invention of the railway? Is this the way people tend to react when most new technological devices first appear? Can they think why people tend to be cautious or suspicious? Are people generally resistant to change?

4. London to Oxford

Age range
Nine to eleven.

Group size
Individuals.

What you need
Photocopiable page 188, advertisements for coach travel today, reference books on Tudor transport.

What to do
Photocopiable page 188 shows an advert for a coach journey between London and Oxford in Tudor times. Ask the children to answer the following questions about the advert:
• What does 'Let them repair to...' mean?
• What do they think the 'Greyhound in Holborn' is?
• How many times a week is the journey made between London and Oxford?
• How long does the journey take?

• On what days of the week is the return journey from Oxford to London undertaken?
• When does the stage begin operating?
• What time does it leave?

Using reference books, can the children draw a picture of what the stage might have looked like?

The second half of the photocopiable page is designed so that the children can write an advertisement for a modern coach journey from London to Oxford. They could use a map to work out the distance from London to Oxford and how long it might take. Better still, they could approach a local bus company and ask them for details of how long it might take.

Further activity
If a local coach company runs a service from the children's home town to Oxford, find out how long it takes, where it stops, and so on. The children could then use this as further evidence of modern transport links, investigating which roads are used and alternative forms of transport available.

5. Cars: good and bad

Age range
Nine to eleven.

Group size
Individuals.

What you need
Reference books on motoring at the beginning of the twentieth century.

What to do
Writing in 1909, F. Masterman wrote in *The Condition of England*: 'Travelling with an incredible rate of speed, motor-cars scramble and smash and shriek along all the rural ways. You can see the evidence of their activity in the dust-laden hedges of the south country roads, a grey mud colour, with no evidence of green, and in the ruined cottage gardens of the south country villages.'

Although this extract may easily refer to the conditions on the roads today, it was written in the early part of the century when there were far fewer cars on the road. Ask the children to investigate what sort of cars would have been on the road in 1909. They could also imagine who F. Masterman was. Why did he hold such views on cars? Where do the children think he lived? They might like to imagine they are F. Masterman writing about cars and the countryside today. What would he say about today's cars? What good and bad effects might he describe?

Further activity
If the children can have access to a copy of a newspaper from the earlier part of the century and one from today, they could look for references to cars in stories and adverts. What conclusions could they draw from such a simple analysis?

BACKGROUND

Domestic life, families and childhood

This subject allows some general themes to be traced across a number of periods.
• Laws affecting the family: in Roman society marriages were monogamous, but divorce was relatively easy. Men could be married at the age of 14 and women at the age of 12. In medieval times, an heiress whose father had died would have become the king's ward. This allowed the king to choose her husband, perhaps to cement a political or economic alliance. By the time the Victorian period arrived property law endowed the husband with his wife's property and this remained the case until the Married Women's Property Act of 1900.

• Toys and leisure activities: children should consider how far toys and leisure were the preserve of particular classes over history. In particular, they could explore how far the concept of 'childhood' is a modern phenomenon.
• Gender roles: this is a particularly important theme for children to pursue and they can use their knowledge of gender roles in modern society and compare these with various periods in history. In slave-owning societies, the wives and daughters of citizens in such places as Greece and Rome were not treated much differently from slaves. It is also the case that throughout British history, children have been treated relatively badly. As women have traditionally been the carers of children, both groups have tended to be neglected by male legislators.

In many levels of Victorian society husbands expected to be obeyed at all times. This often went as far as wives addressing their husbands formally as 'Mr'.
• Housing: much of the knowledge we have about how people lived domestically in the past is derived from what we know about legislation. However, children could use their wider knowledge of periods they have studied to hypothesise on the living conditions of other classes of people such as the rich and middle classes.

Ancient Greece

The citizens of Greece usually lived in houses centred around the public buildings. These houses were built from mud

bricks on a stone foundation and were designed so that they were built round an open courtyard with rooms facing into the courtyard and out into the street. In this courtyard there would usually be a shrine to a household god.

The man played an extremely important part in this household and was seen as being responsible for his wife, children and slaves.

The day in a Greek household would begin extremely early for business and labour. Only the men would go out to work as the women stayed at home doing household tasks, such as caring for the children, preparing the food and mending the clothes, although the women slaves would be responsible for things like washing, cleaning and preparing food. Social life outside the home was almost exclusively for men with the highlight of the day for a man being the visit to the gymnasium.

Children would stay at home until they were six years old. Once they were six, the boys would be sent to school, but the girls were taught at home and their education largely consisted of tuition in domestic affairs. A boy's education would continue until he was 15 and then at age of 18 he became a citizen.

An important family ritual was the eating of the main meal of the day, which was around sunset.

Roman Britain

Towns in Roman Britain were largely built to a common design. They were square or rectangular with straight streets criss-crossing each other like a grid. The whole town was usually surrounded by a large defensive wall and in the centre of the town a forum or market place was situated. Roman houses tended to be long and narrow. However, some of the richer citizens lived in grand villas set in large estates.

Education was divided into three stages determined by age, although the vast majority of children only completed the first stage with very few girls going to school at all. The girls from wealthier families would be educated at home with a tutor, although again the most important lessons were concerned with domestic matters.

Eating and rituals associated with meals were very important to the Romans. Usually, they ate three meals a day with the main meal being eaten in the evening. This meal was preceded by a ritual offering and prayers to the gods. The Romans placed great stress on household gods, known as the *lares*. They believed that the *lares* would protect their homes from evil and the father of the house acted as the priest responsible for the rituals.

Children's games were popular in Roman Britain and these included games which would be recognisable today such as 'Hide-and-seek' and 'Leap-frog'. Indoor and outdoor toys including ball games, were also popular.

Victorian times

Domestic and family life contrasted enormously in Victorian Britain, reflecting the very different social conditions under which people lived. The very poorest people lived in domestic slums and life was squalid and difficult. These families were usually large, even though accommodation would often be confined to one room and with little, if any, sanitation. The diet of these people would be poor and diseases such as smallpox and tuberculosis were rampant. In many families, domestic life had to be built around child labour and children as young as five would be made to work in factories and down the mines.

For wealthy families, the contrast could not have been greater. Here, families were hierarchical with the father placed at the head. Children's behaviour was strictly regulated and rich children would usually be looked after by a nanny or other servants. Their education was begun at home by tutors or governesses before, if you were a boy, being sent away to school. In a sense, the Victorian times saw the beginning of 'childhood' with books and toys being mass produced. However, these were largely confined to the rich.

Teaching plan

Lessons and activities for this section could either be organised according to period or by themes.

Ideally, lessons will combine both approaches as children need some basic period background knowledge before being able to identify contrasts over time.

ACTIVITIES

1. The jar game

Age range
Seven to eleven.

Group size
Small groups.

What you need
A large space such as the assembly hall or playground.

What to do
Young children in Roman Britain liked to play what was known as the 'Jar game'. To play this game one child sat on the ground while the other players came up in turn and pinched her or tapped her. The child on the ground would not be allowed to get up, but if she could grab hold of one of the other children while they were teasing her, the child she had caught had to take her place in the 'jar'. Explain to the children how this game was played and let them play it. Can they add their own adaptations? For example, they could introduce a rule whereby if a teasing child does not touch the child in the jar after 30 seconds, he automatically has to swop places.

Roman children also used to play games which were similar to games played today, such as 'Hide-and-seek', 'Leap-frog', and 'Hopscotch'. 'Blindman's buff' was also played in Roman Britain although rather differently from the way it is played today. Children used to dance around the 'blindman' and tap him with a stick and urge him to catch them.

Further activities
Can the children find out any more about the origins of other games or nursery rhymes? Many of these have their origins in history and provide a useful introduction both to childhood in the past and other features of an historical period. One very good example is the nursery rhyme 'Ring a ring o' roses' which is usually dated to the time of the Black Death, when the first signs of the plague were flu-like symptoms.

2. Girls in Ancient Greece and today

Age range
Nine to eleven.

Group size
Individuals or pairs.

What you need
Reference books on Ancient Greece.

What to do
The lowly position of women and girls in Ancient Greek society was evident from birth with unwanted babies, especially girls, being put out in pots to die in the fields or streets. It was very unusual for girls to go to school although in some wealthy households an educated slave might teach them to read. The majority of their time, however, would be spent learning the domestic

rituals. By the age of 15, a girl would have to give away her toys and marry a man chosen by her father. The wedding was essentially a private ceremony and feast at her father's house, after which she would be taken away with her husband to his home. The duties of a wife would have included such things as managing the money, overseeing the weaving, keeping the wine cool, keeping the corn dry, organising slaves, and keeping the children in order. The women would have a small duty in household religion by making an offering to the gods every morning.

Using this background information, ask the children to compare how far the lives of girls and women have changed from Ancient Greeks to modern society. In particular, they could look at role expectations, using the knowledge they have about family members and contrasting this even with their own experience. This work can lead to some interesting discussions concerning the expectations and behaviour of girls within school.

Allow the children to look at more recent periods including the beginning of the unit on 'Britain since 1930'. The children could consider how far recent factors in the twentieth century have led to women having a very different role in society today. The children could end by making a list of advantages and disadvantages of the roles of women in Greek society and the roles of women today.

Further activity
Ask the children to do a parallel exercise on the role of men. Is it the case that the roles of men over time have stayed much the same? Ask them to examine, in particular, the ancient roles of hunting and fighting; are they still largely the preserve of men today? Also, the children could discuss how far the attitudes of men have remained the same throughout time even though their overt behaviour might have changed.

3. A Roman school and my school

Age range
Nine to eleven.

Group size
Individuals.

What you need
Reference books on the education system in Roman Britain.

What to do
Begin by asking the children to list the main features of their education today. Tell them to include issues such as the schooling system as well as the detailed features of their own school life. They can then contrast their schooling with

the education system in
Roman Britain, which was
divided into three stages. The
first two stages corresponded
roughly to modern primary
and secondary schools and the
third to universities. One
significant difference is that
Roman education was not
compulsory and the vast
majority of children attended
only the first stage of
schooling. It is also true that
education was not free and
very few girls were ever
educated in schools. The
average elementary school,
which roughly corresponded
to a modern primary school,
usually only had ten or twelve
children in it and these
children were taught only to
read and write. Teachers were
not paid enough and often had
to take another job in the
afternoon when the children
had gone home. There were no
formal schools as such and the
teachers had the responsibility
of finding accommodation for
their pupils. This may have
meant working in a corner of a

workshop or even in the
middle of a shopping area; but
wherever lessons were held
there would have been very
little furniture.

The children could then
look at the structure of their
school year including holidays,
when the school year begins,
how many days they spend on
average at school and so on. In
Roman Britain the school year
began in March. Can the
children find out why this was
the case? There were no
weekends but every ninth day
was a holiday and there were
many feast days throughout
the year when the schools
were closed. Ask the children
to look at the length of their
school day and contrast it with
the Roman school day. Lessons
began at dawn and would
finish around mid-day. Then,
in the afternoon after lunch,

there would be two or three
more lessons.

Finally, the children can
think about school discipline.
It is unlikely to be as harsh as
it was in Roman Britain.
Corporal punishment was a
part of everyday life for most
children!

Further activities

It may be possible to arrange a
visit to a Victorian or
Edwardian classroom where
the children can take part in
role-play. If they have
undertaken such a visit can
they then recreate a Roman
classroom, dressing
appropriately and undertaking
the lessons that would have
taken place in a Roman
classroom. They could also

write of their experiences as a Roman child, particularly a British child having to learn Latin and the Roman system of numbers.

4. Victorian books

Age range
Nine to eleven.

Group size
Individuals.

What you need
Extracts from books written in Victorian times, for example, *Black Beauty* by Anna Sewell, *Treasure Island* by Robert Louis Stevenson, *Alice in Wonderland* by Lewis Carroll, and *The Water Babies* by Charles Kingsley.

What to do
Many of the classics of children's literature were written during the Victorian period. However, many children today will not have read these books even though they will probably have seen film adaptations of the stories. Therefore, it is useful to introduce children to these books.
• Read the children extracts from the more dramatic, interesting or amusing parts of the books.
• Read the children part of a book and ask them to dramatise it.
• Watch an extract on video or film of one of the books.
• Listen to a story tape of one of the books.
• Provide shortened or other versions of these stories.
   However, for some children there is no doubt that with teacher promotion they can be encouraged to read these books for themselves. A book such as *Kidnapped* or *Treasure Island* would make an excellent class book which can be read over a number of days or weeks.

Further activities
Ask the children to consider what classics of children's literature from the 1980s or 1990s are likely to be read still in a hundred years time. Which authors will be seen as particularly important by that time? This should provoke the children to discuss what ingredients tend to make a classic book. They might consider whether an extremely popular author like Roald Dahl will still be seen as a classic writer. Is it possible that some of his titles might be seen as classics while others will be forgotten about altogether?

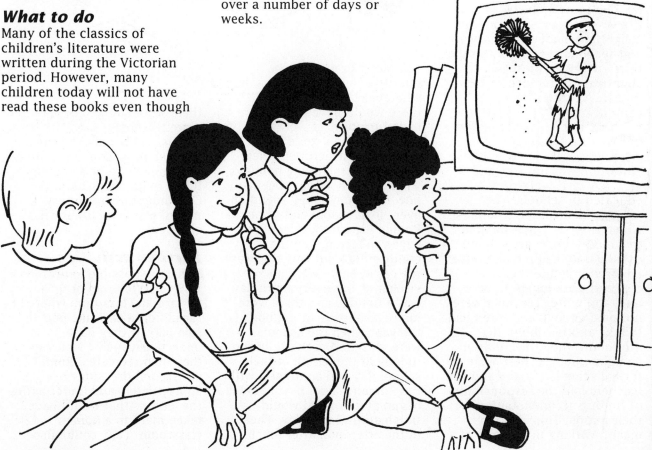

CHAPTER 10

Supplementary study unit B

In the history National Curriculum, category B of the supplementary study units requires that children are taught at least one unit based on local history. This should involve an investigation of an important historical issue and relate local developments to national trends. In particular, three kinds of studies in local history are identified:
• an aspect of the local community over a long period of time;
• an aspect of the local community during a short period of time or the local community's involvement in a particular event;
• an aspect of the local community which illustrates developments taught in other study units.

Where teachers choose to teach two study units in local history, they should involve the study of different types of local history.

The activities described in this chapter are intended to provide suggestions which may well encompass more than one lesson.

An aspect of the local community over a long period of time

To undertake this study, it is necessary to choose a theme about which there is likely to be evidence from different periods of time. This could include:

• education;
• immigration and emigration;
• religion;
• leisure;
• shopping;
• people at work and industry.

When a theme has been chosen, it is likely that it will be necessary to make contact with museums, libraries and sites of historical interest within the area to provide resources. As far as possible, allow the children to research a subject for themselves, although it might be difficult for them to find or access sources easily. It may be necessary to interpret some of the sources for the children before encouraging them to pursue more advanced research. As you are looking over a period of time, it is often worthwhile to contact the local history society who might be able to provide background information on the theme being studied.

ACTIVITIES

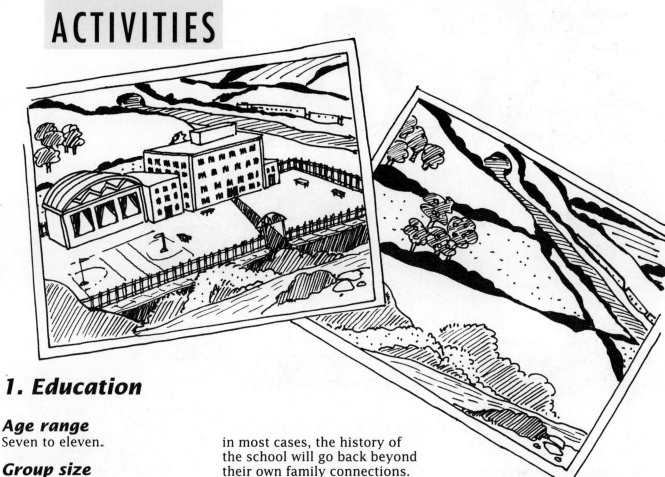

1. Education

Age range
Seven to eleven.

Group size
Individuals, small groups or the whole class.

What you need
Local records, local history books, school records such as registers, log books and so on.

What to do
Education over a long period is an excellent theme to study because children can begin with their own experiences of being in school. Begin by asking them to describe highlights of their time in school, putting dates or years beside each of them. If they have had older brothers or sisters in the school, they will be able to provide a family link beyond the time when they began in the school. However, in most cases, the history of the school will go back beyond their own family connections.

Ask the children to describe how they could find out about the past history of their school. Tell them to think about the day-to-day records which are kept in school and ask them to consider the advantages and disadvantages of different sources, for example, the head teacher's log books compared with the school attendance registers. Invite the children to suggest other sources of evidence outside the school which they could use, for example, the recollections of previous pupils, references to the school in the local newspapers and so on.

The whole project will become particularly interesting if education beyond the history of the school is looked at. Did the school replace another school? If so, does evidence for the other school still exist? What records exist locally? What can be found out about the pupils and teachers of the former school? From other secondary sources, can the children build up a picture of what life in school would have been like at about that time? If the school is in an estate which, itself, has a limited history, what can they find out about the use of land before the houses were built. If it was farmland, who owned it and how would their children have been educated?

2. Immigration and emigration

Age range
Nine to eleven.

Group size
Individuals, small groups and the whole class.

What you need
Local census material or parish records.

What to do
Children will often assume that the community they live in has always been the way it is, with the kind of people it has in it. This can prove to be an interesting area of study as children see that the life and culture of a community has evolved over time and is continuing to evolve as new people arrive and others leave.

Begin by looking at the records from as far back as you can. Remind the children that they need to be looking for clues such as surnames which might refer to jobs that people did or where they have come from.

Ask the children to look at family connections. Are the succeeding generations represented in the records or is there evidence of new people coming in? Is the area where the school is located near a point at which newcomers have arrived, for example, on the coast?

The children could then also look at the development of local industries in the area. Where did their workforces come from? Was local labour employed or did people have to come in from different parts of the country? Do any local customs, festivals or street names reflect the influence of the newcomers? The demise of industries has also led to emigration over time. Where did people go? What did they do?

The children could also investigate how far there is evidence in their area of people coming from abroad into their community. Why did people come? What problems did they face? What have their families chosen to do? What influences have there been on the local community?

Finally to bring their study right up to date, they could look at the children in their own class. How many children were born elsewhere? Why did families move to the area? If there is comparable data from ten years ago, have there been changes in the pattern? If so, why?

BACKGROUND

An aspect of the local community during a short period of time

Such a study is likely to be of most benefit if it is related to a national event which has had an impact locally. There is also an advantage in choosing an event within the twentieth century as it is likely that eyewitness evidence could be drawn upon. Subjects in this category could include:
• the Second World War and the local community;
• the Queen's coronation (or Silver Jubilee);
• a local disaster such as a mining accident;
• the local community in the 1960s (or any other decade in the recent past).

Again, it will be necessary to gather evidence and information. However, greater use can be made of the children themselves as they can be invited to bring in artefacts, photographs and newspaper clippings from the period concerned. Contact should also be made with parents and grandparents who may have eyewitness accounts or memories to share.

ACTIVITIES

1. A local event

Age range
Seven to eleven.

Group size
Individuals, small groups or the whole class.

What you need
Documents, photographs, artefacts, newspaper reports, eyewitness accounts related to a major event in the local area.

What to do
It is very useful to look at the history of an event which happened locally which had no direct national parallel, for example:
• a major disaster;
• the opening of a new factory or the coming of a new industry;
• a major sporting or cultural event.

Again, it is necessary to gather together evidence and information about the event. This activity differs from the following one in that here there is a greater opportunity for the children to look at causes. What caused the event to happen? Do people agree on the causes? Could the event have happened differently?

The children could also look at the event itself. How far are eyewitness accounts and memories biased by how the event affected different people? Look too at consequences. Does the local community agree on the consequences? Are the consequences all 'good' or 'bad'? This is an excellent opportunity for children to exercise their historical judgement based on the evidence in front of them.

2. War!

Age range
Eight to eleven.

Group size
Individuals, small groups, or the whole class.

What you need
Artefacts such as ration books, gas masks and so on; photographs, local newspapers, eyewitness accounts of people who lived through the period.

What to do
Begin by providing a time-line of the Second World War. You could devote a panel or space on the classroom wall to each of the seven years from 1939 through to 1945. You could also provide an overview of the main events of these years or you could see how far these events can be discovered by finding out what was happening locally.

Choose particular events such as the Battle of Britain, rationing, schooling, evacuation, bombing, the Blitz and VE day. What evidence can be gathered locally about these events? How valuable are eyewitness accounts and memories, particularly so long after the event? What other evidence do the children think they need in order to obtain a more complete picture?

Ask the children to try and build up a picture of what life was like during the war from one of their witnesses.

Finally, ask the children to compare national events against what happened in their area. If their area was not subject to the Blitz, is there a particular reason for this, for example, was their area considered of little strategic, industrial or military importance?

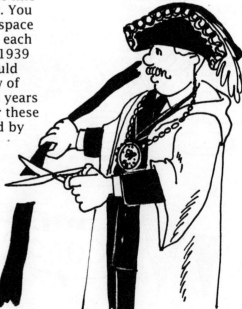

BACKGROUND

An aspect of the local community which illustrates developments taught in other units

The choice of subject is substantial and depends on where a school is located. Examples of subjects would include:

- the Roman influence;
- Tudor and Stuart buildings;
- the effect on the local community of the industrial revolution;
- computer technology and our community;
- shipbuilding in our area;
- farms;
- local churches.

This local history dimension could either be taught as part of the work on another study unit (for example, Victorian Britain could be taught by looking at major issues and their effects locally) or, it could be taught as a discrete subject.

ACTIVITIES

1. Farms

Age range
Seven to eleven.

Group size
Individuals, small groups or the whole class.

What you need
Documents, records and maps, relating to farms in the local community.

What to do
Even in the most built up area it is likely that farms previously existed in the area at some point in the past. As part of their work on the supplementary study unit 'Food and farming', the children could begin by using local maps from the past which identify where the farms were situated. Is there evidence to indicate who owned them? What was grown on them? What led to the farm's disappearance if this happened?

Where a farm has existed for a substantial period of time, seek permission to visit it and talk to the farmer. How long has the farmer farmed the land? How has it been organised? What changes have been made over time and why?

CHAPTER 11

Supplementary study unit C

The activities in this section are based on with the study units concerned with non-european societies of the past. At least one of these units will be studied during Key stage 2 and they should:
• involve study from a variety of perspectives, for example, political, economic, social and religious;
• introduce children to the study of archaeological evidence;
• cover the everyday lives of men and women.

Potentially these study units will allow children to gain access to important aspects of world history. However, in practice, beyond Ancient Egypt, teachers will find it extremely difficult to tackle these subjects in depth because of the lack of resources and books available.

Therefore, it may be appropriate to tackle these units as shorter, week-long topics.

Ancient Egypt is the first topic covered in this section and it is designed to focus on the way of life of the Ancient Egyptians. The focus should be on food and farming, people and society, religious beliefs, culture and science and technology.

The second topic is on the origins and development of Mesopotamia and focuses on life in Mesopotamia, its rules and states, religion, science and technology. It will also serve as a useful introduction to looking at and using archaeological evidence.

The Assyrian Empire is the subject of the third topic in this section. It covers the period from the eighth century BC until the fall of Nineveh in 612BC. The focus here is on everyday life, culture, religion and science and technology.

The study unit on the Indus Valley from its origins, in approximately 2500BC to its decline around 1700BC. It should be pointed out that there are few reference materials suitable for children on this subject which means that children will have to investigate the contribution made by archaeology in understanding the past.

The Mayan people from AD250 to 900 are the subject of the fifth study unit. The focus is on how the Maya lived, their religion and scientific and artistic achievements. The final subject unit focuses on the West African civilisation during the period from the middle of the fifteenth to the middle of the seventeenth centuries. The context should include how the Benin were ruled, how they lived, their culture and their relations with other countries and peoples. Again, resources on the Benin are limited.

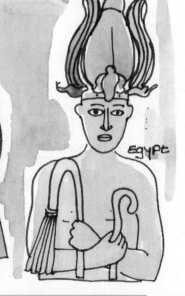

Maya

Mesopotamia

Indus

Egypt

BACKGROUND

Ancient Egypt

Egypt was one of the world's first great civilisations. It had the advantage of being protected from its enemies by deserts, yet it was able to produce food in plentiful supply in its fertile soil around the Nile.

The first civilisation emerged in Lower Egypt around the Nile approximately 7000 years ago, followed closely by another kingdom in Upper Egypt. Little is known about these kingdoms and the subsequent single kingdom

they became with Heliopolis as its capital. Around 3000BC, Menes, the ruler of the Upper Kingdom, conquered the Lower Kingdom. He became pharaoh and his rule was known as the Old Kingdom or the Pyramid Age. Great pyramids were built at Saqqara and Giza. The kingdom had its capital in Memphis.

The Old Kingdom eventually broke up and there followed a period of virtual anarchy. Eventually, however, the Middle Kingdom emerged around 2050BC. The capital of this Middle Kingdom was at Thebes. This became a powerful and important city in which vast temples were built, canals established and trade with Crete, Cyprus and Lebanon flourished.

The New Kingdom emerged in 1500BC ruled over by a series of strong pharaohs including Amenhotep I and Thotmes I. This kingdom soon became an Empire with a powerful army.

However after Rameses II, who came to the throne in 1304BC, there followed a period of decline. The Empire was lost in 669BC, when the country was invaded by the Assyrians. Then Alexander (the Great) placed it under Greek rule before, eventually, Egypt became a province of the Roman Empire in 31BC.

Throughout the thousands of years when Egypt was a great civilisation, a number of elements remained constant. There was a small group of leaders, headed by the Pharaoh, who ruled, and the rest of the people were essentially workers – including craftsmen such as scribes and labourers who worked in the fields and quarries.

The Egyptians believed in many gods. The greatest was Ra, the Sun-god, but there were others including Osiris, the god of the Nile and Hathor, the goddess of love, happiness and music. Additionally, the Egyptians believed in many local gods who protected towns and communities. They believed in life after death, which is clearly shown by the trouble they took to preserve their dead.

Egyptian life and society recognised the critical role played by the Nile in their prosperity. Egyptian farmers recognised that they were dependent on the banks of the Nile being covered with water to create a rich soil. This overflow from the Nile was known as the 'Inundation'. Once it was over, the farmers broke up the soil and ploughed it and sowed it. A series of dykes and channels was devised in order to retain as much of the water as possible to irrigate their crops.

The Egyptians were also lawmakers and administrators. They believed that the world had been created by the gods to reflect a principle of truth and justice called Maet. Their society was, in many ways, humane; best exemplified in the treatment of women and slaves, both of whom had legal rights.

Key dates

The following dates are still the subject of debate among historians and archaeologists and are subject to alterations as new finds are discovered.
3118BC: Menes united Upper and Lower Egypt.
3000–2100BC: the Old Kingdom was formed.
2650BC: the death of Zoser, for whom the first pyramid was built.
2050–1630BC: the Middle Kingdom was formed.
1567–1085BC: the New Kingdom was formed.
1504–1450BC: the reign of Tuthmosis, who created a vast empire for Egypt.
669BC: Assyrians invaded Egypt.
332BC: Alexander (the Great) invaded Egypt.
31BC: Egypt became a Roman province.

Teaching plan

A series of lessons and activities on Ancient Egypt could be organised as follows.
• The three kingdoms.
• Food and farming.
• The Pyramids and the religion of the Egyptians.
• Social and family life.
• Egypt at war.
• Society, law and administration.
• Writing.

ACTIVITIES

1. Making papyrus

Age range
Seven to nine.

Group size
Individuals or pairs.

What you need
Sugar paper, polythene sheeting, wallpaper paste (without fungicide), brush, wooden board, bricks, paint, reference books on the pyramids.

What to do
Begin by asking the children to tear the sugar paper into strips approximately 30cm in length. They should lay them out vertically on top of the polythene sheeting and cover them with wallpaper paste. They must then lay another layer of strips on top, but this time they should be set out horizontally to the first. Repeat this process about six times and then finally, place another sheet of polythene on top and weight the whole lot down with a board and bricks.

The children should then leave it for a week or so, until the paper has bonded to form one sheet.

Finally, they could use reference books to research the kinds of paintings which appeared in the tombs of the pharaohs and paint their papyrus accordingly.

Further activity
Ask the children to discover what materials the Egyptians used to make papyrus and ask them to investigate how paper is made today.

2. Hieroglyphics

Age range
Seven to nine.

Group size
Individuals.

What you need
Reference books on Ancient Egypt which provide background information on hieroglyphics, paper, pens.

What to do
Egyptian writing was largely based around small pictures called *hieroglyphs*. Initially, pictures were used to depict

objects and then the pictures came to represent sounds. There were several hundred signs. Ask the children to use the reference books to see if they can find out what some of the signs mean.

Ask the children to devise their own stories, perhaps about Egyptian gods, using hieroglyphs. They will need to use as many nouns as possible, although they could write the conjunctions in English. Better still, they could devise their own symbols for words like 'a' and 'the'. They could then provide a key and see if friends could read their stories.

Further activity
The scribes were important people in ancient Egypt. Provide some background information about them, telling the children, for example, that training started at the age of five, and they practised their work on stone and pottery. The children can then write a story imagining they are scribes. This should include:
• how they spend their day;
• who they meet;
• what instruments they make;
• what problems they encounter;
• what work they write about.

3. An Egyptian court

Age range
Nine to eleven.

Group size
The whole class.

What you need
Lengths of fabric, make-up, reference books to provide costume information.

What to do
As Egyptian society developed, an administrative structure was created to keep records and dispense justice. The chief minister of the pharaoh was called the vizier, who oversaw agriculture and held a high court of justice. Ask the children to dress up as Egyptians and create a court of justice. The vizier must listen to a case, for example, of village chiefs who had failed to collect taxes or of soldiers who had failed to look after their equipment. Other children can act as the accused, the accusers and scribes. The vizier must listen to all the evidence as the case is presented and then pronounce his judgement and the sentence.

Further activity
Ask the children to investigate the social structure of Ancient Egypt. Who formed the upper class of society along with the vizier? Who formed the bulk of the population? What opportunities were there for advancement?

Mesopotamia

'Mesopotamia' is a Greek word meaning 'land between the rivers' (the rivers are the Tigris and Euphrates in Western Asia). In general terms, Mesopotamia occupied the greater part of what is now Iraq.

There is evidence of settlement in Mesopotamia as far back as about 10,000BC. The favourable climate of the region allowed people to move from being wandering hunter-gatherers to settle as farmers working on the land. Even at this early stage, trade with other regions flourished.

Technologically, Mesopotamia was a sophisticated society with well-developed irrigation techniques and high quality pottery.

In approximately 3000BC the city-kingdoms grew up in southern Mesopotamia in a region occupied by the Sumerian people. Ur was the major city and among the others were Lagash, Larsa, Kish and Erech. These city-kingdoms were each ruled over by a king who was also believed to be the earthly representative of the local god.

However, the rule of the individual city-kingdoms did not last long as Sargon, the ruler of Akkad, a region further north, had conquered all of the local rulers by 2500BC. This dynasty ruled for a few centuries, but by 2112BC, the city-kingdoms had re-established themselves, with Ur becoming the most powerful once again. The greatest ruler of all was King Ur-Nammu, founder of the Third Dynasty of Ur.

Throughout the Third Dynasty, religion played a central role in the life of both kings and people. Gods were seen to be involved in all aspects of life including laws and the distribution of food. The will of the gods was interpreted by high priests reading the omens. The gods were worshipped in the *ziggurat* or temple. This was believed to be the dwelling place of Nannar, the moon god. However, there were also

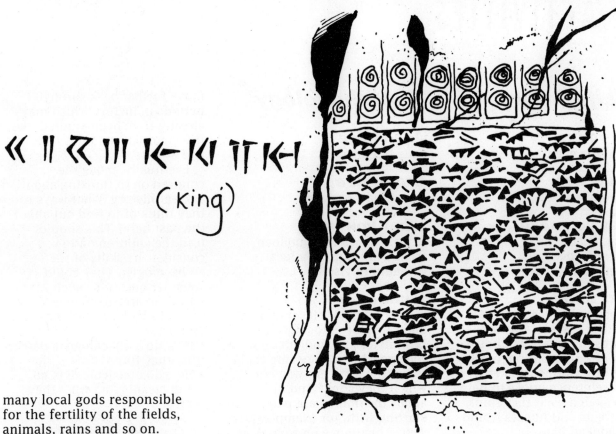

《 ‖ ⟨ ⫴ ⊩ ⊩ ⫴ ⟨

(`king)

many local gods responsible for the fertility of the fields, animals, rains and so on.

In about 2000BC, this great kingdom was destroyed by a tribe called the Amorites. From this tribe emerged Hammurabi, another great ruler. He became a great law maker and ruler from his capital Babylon. He issued many decrees and laws and these covered subjects as diverse as accidental death and the role of women in society. In addition, the cuneiform script developed which saw writing move from being in the form of pictures to a series of lines. Writing was done with a wedge-shaped stylus on a tablet of clay.

After Hammurabi died, the Kassites overran the valley and Babylon was captured. At this stage, and for the next 1000 years, the focus moved to the Assyrian empire.

Key dates

All the dates given here are very approximate although the archaeological evidence from this period is quite substantial.
10,000BC: The development of civilisation in Mesopotamia.
4000BC: Civilisation in Sumeria.
3000BC: Foundation of the city of Ur and the development of writing.
2600BC: The First Dynasty of Ur.
2500BC: The Second Dynasty of Ur.
2300BC: Unification of Babylonia under Akkadian rule.
2100BC: The revival of the Sumerian rule and the Third Dynasty of Ur.
2000BC: Hammurabi, King of Babylon.
1600BC: Hurrians, Kassites and Mitanni migrate into Mesopotamia and become the rulers.
1500BC: Rise of Assyria, northern Mesopotamia.

Teaching plan

A series of lessons and activities on Mesopotamia could be organised as follows.
• Using archaeological evidence to discover Mesopotamia.
• Religion in Mesopotamia.
• Technology and writing in Mesopotamia.
• Hammurabi and his law making society.

ACTIVITIES

1. Life in Ur

Age range
Seven to eleven.

Group size
Individuals.

What you need
Photocopiable page 189, reference books on Mesopotamia.

What to do
Photocopiable page 189 describes some of the major features of streets and houses in Ur. Ask the children to use these descriptions and any other reference books to help them sketch what they think the streets and houses would have looked like.

Further activity
Ask the children to consider what evidence there might be to find out how people lived in Ur. Is it likely that this evidence would cover all sections of society? If not, why not?

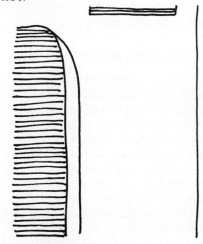

2. Archaeology

Age range
Nine to eleven.

Group size
Individuals or pairs.

What you need
Historical artefacts on loan from a museum or a local museum to visit.

What to do
A brief study of Mesopotamia allows children to consider how historians find out about the past. Begin by asking them to list the different ways in which they could find out about the immediate past, starting with, for example, last year. Then move on to look at the past within the lifetime of their parents and grandparents. You can then move further back through periods in history which may already have been studied like the Victorians and the Tudors and Stuarts.

Eventually, move the children on to thinking about ancient history. What ways can they think of to find out about the past here? This should lead the children on to consider the skills of the archaeologist. They could consider questions such as:
• How do archaeologists know where to look for historical artefacts?
• How do archaeologists date what they find?
• How do archaeologists go about cleaning up what they find?

• What are the dangers of relying exclusively on archaeological evidence – what does it *not* tell us?

If the children can visit a local museum, so much the better, because they can talk to staff about the oldest objects in the different collections. They could discover where and when they were found, who found them and how the museum came to own them.

Further activities

If there is a local archaeological society in the area, ask a member to come and talk to the children. Using their own knowledge of the area perhaps the children could suggest appropriate places to dig. Ask them to consider what archaeology from our society might survive 2000 years and allow historians of the future to build up a picture of how we lived.

3. The law maker

Age range
Nine to eleven.

Group size
Individuals or pairs.

What you need
Reference books about the laws passed during the reign of Hammurabi, King of Babylon.

What to do
Hammurabi's reign, around 2000BC, was a time of great law making. He ordered all the laws, both old and new, to be engraved on a large stone and placed in the temple of Marduk, god of Babylon. These laws were also made known throughout the land.

Laws were passed on many things, including the following subjects:
• the role of women;
• the rights of slaves;
• the duties of children to attend school;
• rules for trading and the production of goods;
• stealing;
• murder;
• accidental death.

Given what the children know of ancient societies, ask them to write down what they think the laws of Hammurabi would have been like. Then ask them to consider the laws concerning each of the above areas during other periods of history they have studied. The children could then answer some more general questions, again based on their knowledge of different historical periods:
• Why have societies passed an increasing number of laws through time?
• Have laws become more humane over time? If so, why?
• Why have the rights of individuals become so important?
• Why, during different periods of history, were people treated differently under the law (for example, slaves and freemen)?
• How are laws made today?
• What have people done in the past when they have not agreed with laws?

Further activity
Ask the children to look at the rules which govern their own life in school. Do they have any underlying principles (for example, 'treat others as you would want to be treated yourself')? Who makes the rules? What happens if they are broken?

Assyria

The first date at which it can be confidently said that the Assyrians were living in Assur is about 2000BC. Assur was the northern-most part of the River Tigris, although it was also the name of the local god. Historically, the Assyrians were originally under the control of Akkadian and Ur. However, as they were fighters and traders they had picked up many skills from the Babylonians.

From about 850BC, the Assyrians began to conquer large parts of the Middle East. They used highly sophisticated military tactics, including horse-drawn chariots and spearmen to protect their archers. In addition, they also developed military technology such as siege towers and battering rams. Essentially, they were pillagers who carried off the fruits of their conquests to their capital city, Nineveh, or their other great city, Nimrud.

The great period of their conquests from about 800BC to 600BC was dominated by six Assyrian kings. Ashurnasirpal II ruled from 883 to 859BC. He was a temple builder, who expanded the empire to the north and the east. He was succeeded by Shalmaneser III who ruled from 858 to 824BC. He continued the expansion of the empire, defeating a coalition of Syrian and Palestinian armies.

However, by the end of his reign, a rebellion had been led against the king from the cities of Assyria and Babylon. The next great king Tiglath-Pileser III ruled from 745 to 727BC. He reinforced the army, invaded Palestine and captured the cities of Jerusalem and Damascus. By the time of Surgon II, 722–705BC, the empire consisted of over 700 provinces. The empire was further enlarged by Sennacherib who ruled from 704 to 681BC. But it was Assur-bani-pal who was the most powerful of all these kings. He ruled from 668 to 626BC. He invaded Egypt as far as Thebes and, although he had to endure a subsequent civil war when his brother turned against him, he eventually captured Babylon in 648BC. He was also a scholar and administrator and much of the literature of the time was written on to stone tablets.

However, almost as suddenly as the empire grew up, it collapsed. It was attacked by the Chaldeans who captured Babylon before joining an alliance with the Medes and attacking Nineveh in 612BC.

Key dates

1200BC: Assurdan I beccame king and Assur was made the capital city.

1100BC: Tiglath-Pileser was king and Assyria was attacked on all sides by Aramaeans and Guitans.
900BC: Assyria became the centre of an empire with Nineveh as the capital city. Babylonian religious cults spread into Assyria. Six kings followed over the next two centuries.
883–859BC: Ashurnasirpal II.
858–824BC: Shalmaneser III.
745–727BC: Tiglath-Pileser III.
722–705BC: Sargon II.
704–681BC: Sennacherib.
669–631BC: Assur-bani-pal.
700BC: Invasion of Egypt and the sack of Babylon.
612BC: Medes destroyed Nineveh.

Teaching plan

A series of lessons and activities on Assyria could be organised as follows.
• The six great kings.
• The Assyrians as a military power.
• Assyrian buildings.
• Science, technology and culture in Assyria.

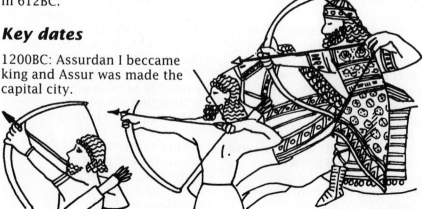

ACTIVITIES

1. A grand frieze

Age range
Seven to nine.

Group size
Groups of four children.

What you need
Reference books on Assyria, frieze paper, paper, felt-tipped pens, adhesive.

What to do
The Assyrian kings built many fine palaces and temples. The courtyards of these palaces were often decorated with huge carved friezes which stretched for many metres. These often depicted great scenes from Assyrian history or myths. Using the frieze paper as a background, ask the children to make a scene from the history of the Assyrian Empire. They should draw, colour in and cut out individual figures and scenes. When each group has done its scene, they could all be stuck on to the frieze paper and displayed around the classroom. The scenes which could be depicted would include:
• the building of a great palace;
• the archers, spearmen and chariots in battle;
• the attack on Damascus using the battering rams and siege machines;
• the six great kings of the empire;
• the building up of great libraries and books;
• the grand buildings of Assyria.

Further activities
Ask the children to look at other great depictions from history such as the Bayeux Tapestry or they could look at how simple art such as cave paintings can provide an insight into the past.

The children could then go on to create a grand frieze for their school. What elements would they draw to represent their school?

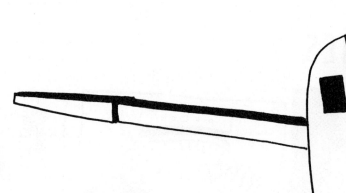

2. Military technology

Age range
Eight to eleven.

Group size
Individuals or pairs.

What you need
Wood dowling, cotton reels or wheels, adhesive, strong elastic, thin card, toy soldier figures.

What to do
The Assyrians were one of the first people to harness technology for military advantage. Their archers used the protection of shields to deliver a frightening barrage of arrows. Using the toy soldier figures to represent the archers, can the children use the thin card and dowling to make a set of shields which could then be deployed defensively around their figures?

Ask the children to experiment with different ways of organising the shields. Which formation provides better protection for the soldiers? The Assyrians also used horse-drawn carriages to give themselves mobility in battle. Using the materials provided, can the children make such a chariot?

It was in heavy military technology that the Assyrians made most strides. They used battering rams and siege machines. Can the children draw up plans for their own designs of such devices and then use the materials to build their own? Set them some targets, for example:
• the siege machines must be able to stand up against a wall and include a means by which small figures could go up it;
• the battering ram must be able to knock a hole in a piece of card.

Further activity
Ask the children to trace developments in military technology through time. They could investigate the means by which artillery is used to create a tactical advantage in war or they could look at how the police use their shields in different ways during riots.

3. Stories and legends of the past

Age range
Nine to eleven.

Group size
Individuals.

What you need
Reference books on Assyria.

What to do
Assur-bani-pal, the last of the great kings of Assyria, collected over 20,000 stone tablets to form a huge library. The stories and legends told on these stones included those relating to the creation of the world and the great flood.

Ask the children to devise their own stories which they could pretend were old Assyrian legends. Themes could include:
• Tiglath-Pileser III and the creation of a strong army;
• the building of the great city of Nineveh;
• the capture of Egypt.

When the children have written their stories, they could dramatise them and perform them to the rest of the class.

Further activity
The children could devise legends relating to the present day depicting modern themes such as the invention of television or the first pop music and dancing.

BACKGROUND

The Indus Valley

The Indus Valley is the earliest known urban culture of the Indian sub-continent, in what is modern-day Punjab and Pakistan. Its existence was first discovered by archaeologists in the 1920s. Since then, archaeological interpretation has concluded that the society was in existence from approximately 2500BC to 1700BC.

The civilisation consisted of two large cities, Harappa and Mohenjo-daro, as well as over 100 smaller towns and villages. Archaeologists up until now have been unable to discover what led to the growth of such a sophisticated and successful civilisation. It was a literate civilisation, with a written script of between 250 and 500 characters. However, interpretation has proved difficult and what scripts remain have proven difficult to decipher. Therefore, it is hard to find out much about the political organisation of the society, or features such as the religion, domestic life and social culture.

There is evidence that the civilisation flourished by developing irrigated agriculture which allowed for sophisticated farming of crops such as wheat, barley and peas. There is also evidence that domesticated animals such as dogs, cats and fowl were kept. The cities were largely similar in design, with the buildings being constructed of brick with the most important ones built outside the cities, overlooking them. Little remains as evidence to tell us more about how the people lived, but relics of domestic implements such as bowls and cups have been found.

Art remains the most interesting and available source of evidence about the civilisation of the Indus Valley. The best known artefacts that have been discovered are seals, which were generally made of steatite. These seals were extremely decorative with carvings of wild animals, fantastic creatures, and even humans. Other finds include some stone sculptures and small terracotta figures.

It is generally accepted that around 1500BC invaders destroyed the two major cities of Harappa and Mohenjo-daro. There is, however, little evidence of who these invaders were or why the Indus Valley civilisation lasted for such a short time. It has been speculated that the irrigation techniques of the people proved to be less successful as time went on and that as a consequence floods became more severe, rendering the soil infertile.

In conclusion it can be said that the archaeological evidence available concerning the Indus Valley presents an interesting insight into an ancient civilisation, but leaves many questions unanswered.

Key dates and teaching plan

Given the paucity of archaeological evidence, it is not possible to provide a list of key dates for this study unit. The two dates referred to above are the only dates that can be given with any degree of certainty.

Also, the limited amount of material available on this subject means that any teaching plan will consist largely of examinations of the archaeological evidence available. However, there are ample opportunities to make use of this study unit as a means to discovering more about how historians draw conclusions about the past.

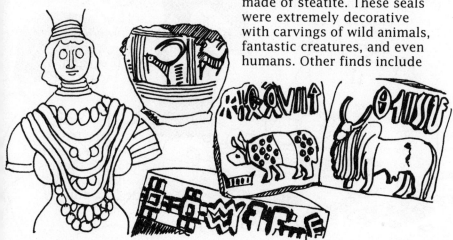

ACTIVITIES

1. Indus Valley jewellery

Age range
Eight to eleven.

Group size
Individuals.

What you need
Scrap materials such as cloth, beads, sequins and so on.

What to do
Many fine artefacts from the Indus Valley civilisation, made of metal and stone, have been found. In addition items of jewellery such as necklaces, bracelets, ear-rings and rings made of jade and onyx and precious metals such as gold, have also been discovered. Jewellery appears to have been made in many different shapes and sizes and depicts humans, animals and other, fantastic, creatures. Ask the children to design their own jewellery using the scrap materials. To what use do they think such jewellery was put? Was it necessarily only for decorative purposes or might it have had some religious symbolism?

Further activity
Ask the children to look at different periods of history to see how jewellery and other fashions have developed over time. Again, this could be brought right up to the present as the children look at the most modern developments in jewellery. They could also consider how far modern-day jewellery has been influenced by past times and cultures.

2. Discovery!

Age range
Nine to eleven.

Group size
Pairs.

What you need
No special requirements.

What to do
All that we know about the Indus Valley comes from archaeological discovery. Put the children into pairs and ask them to imagine that they are archaeologists working in the 1920s in the area where the major discoveries were first made. The children could make up a short drama which explores the reactions of the archaeologists as they made their first discoveries about the Indus Valley civilisation. They should think about including:
• why they were digging in that area in the first place;
• what initial items they found;
• what their early judgements were of what they found;
• how they proceeded to investigate further;
• what evidence they used to draw their conclusions;
• how they displayed their finds and let the world know about them.

The children could also use an atlas to discover what the climate and physical geography of the area of the Indus Valley is like. They could also consider what methods of excavation would have been

used in the 1920s and what difficulties the archaeologists would have been faced with as the expedition took place. Can the children find out about different methods of dating objects that were used at that time and compare these with more modern approaches such as carbon dating?

Further activities
Ask the children to contact local museums or universities to find out what modern methods are used in archaeological expeditions. In particular, they could investigate how archaeologists make judgements about the age of their discoveries. They could also find examples of how, as techniques for finding out about the past have become more sophisticated, an interpretation of the past has changed. Ask the children to look at how far judgements about timescales are merely approximations; for example

the two dates of the Indus Valley civilisation, 2500BC and 1700BC – are these simply rough estimates or are they well substantiated by documentary, archaeological or scientific evidence?

3. Why do civilisations decline?

Age range
Nine to eleven.

Group size
Individuals.

What you need
No special requirements.

What to do
One of the great mysteries of the Indus Valley civilisation is how and why it declined. It is probably quite difficult for young children to imagine the reasons why an ancient society might go into decline.

However, with older children it is worth asking them if they can think of any reasons. They might suggest things like war, invasion, flood, change in economic circumstances and so on. Point out to the children that no firm conclusions can be drawn about the decline of the Indus Valley civilisation because the archaeological evidence is not there to support any particular view.

Further activity
You may then want to look at other examples of decline in civilisations in history, both ancient and modern. There is much better information available about the decline of other civilisations and societies, which the children may well have already studied as part of their National Curriculum history programme, for example those of the Anglo-Saxons, Romans and the Ancient Egyptians. It is also worth looking at a very modern parallel such as the break up of the USSR. The children have easy access to newspapers and books on this subject and they may well also have some recollections of what major factors contributed to this decline.

The Maya

Work on the Maya can be easily related to work on 'Exploration and encounters 1450 to 1550'. Even though this core study unit concentrates on the Aztec civilisation, it will allow for contrasts and comparisons between the Aztecs and the Maya.

The Maya were Meso-American Indians who occupied an almost continuous territory in what is, today, southern Mexico, Guatemala and northern Belize. As early as 1500BC, the Maya had settled in villages and developed a primitive system of agriculture. However, the great development in Mayan society began around 200AD. By this time, their settlements had developed into large cities, particularly in the lowlands where temples, pyramids and palaces, built from quarried stone, were all common sights. At its height, the Mayan civilisation consisted of over 40 cities including Tikal, Uaxactun and Riobec, all of which had substantial populations.

The Mayan civilisation was extremely sophisticated. It had a system of hieroglyphic writing and a very accurate calendar. This calendar was calculated on the basis of 365 days, although it was divided into 18 months of 20 days each. The days that remained were seen as an unlucky period. The Maya had two major ways of calculating the year – one was based on religious feast days and the other made reference to the origins of the Mayan civilisation. In addition, the Maya were also extremely interested in mathematics. They developed positional notation using base 20 and they introduced the concept of zero.

Their religion was based on a pantheon of nature gods such as the sun, the moon, the rain and crops such as corn. The priests led by the Hunab Ku, were extremely important as they were responsible for carrying out the sacred rituals. Throughout the great period of the Mayan civilisation, religion was extremely important.

Politically, little is known of how Mayan society was organised, although it is believed that the cities were largely independent states ruled by the Halach Uinich, which was a hereditary office. Historians also believe that the Mayan society was rigidly stratified with the priests the most important class.

The Maya also had a sophisticated system of agriculture and were able to grow many different crops. They were also great hunters, hunting animals such as armadillos and wild pigs. However, they kept few domesticated animals.

Little is known about the decline of the Mayan civilisation, although historians generally agree that the great period of civilisation was divided into two major parts. The early classic period ran from, approximately, 250AD to 600AD and the late classic period ran from then until 900AD. It is generally believed that the Mayan society declined quite simply because the people moved elsewhere. In fact, there is little or no evidence to show that the society was subject to any major disasters such as war or famine.

Teaching plan

A series of lessons and activities on the Maya could be organised as follows.
• How the people lived.
• Religion of the Maya.
• Scientific, technological and artistic achievements.

ACTIVITIES

1. The nature of the gods

Age range
Seven to nine.

Group size
Individuals.

What you need
No special requirements.

What to do
The Mayan society had many legends and stories based around their nature gods such as the god of the sun or the god of the moon. Begin by asking the children why it is that in many ancient civilisations the elements or the stars or heavenly bodies were seen as god-like figures. Having discussed this, the children can write their own legend based around one of the nature gods. This could have as its theme:
• the creation of the world;
• the coming into existence of the sun or the moon;
• how the natural element considered (for example, water or fire) played a role in the life of the Maya;
• what could happen if people behaved wrongly or failed to worship the gods;
• how the gods could intervene in Mayan society.

The children could then illustrate their stories using a variety of art materials. Perhaps if they had written a story about the sun, they could write it out in a sun shape or if they had written about water, in a raindrop shape, and display it in a book of myths and legends about the Mayan people.

Further activity
The creation story appears in many ancient civilisations. If the children are not familiar with such stories, ask them to find out how the creation is recounted within various religions, such as Christianity or Islam.

2. Mayan maths

Age range
Nine to eleven.

Group size
Individuals.

What you need
Photocopiable sheet 190.

What to do
Photocopiable page 190 provides a break down of the Mayan number system. It also provides some activities for the children to carry out using these numbers, working in base 20. This gives the children an opportunity to work in other bases such as base 4, base 5 or base 6. It also allows them to consider what advantages there are in working in our mathematical system which is based around base 10. Ask the children to consider the importance of using zero in a number system. What would happen if the number system did not have a zero? Could the children devise a simple number system that does not depend on zero?

Further activity
The history of mathematics is an extremely interesting subject and could provide a very good mini-theme in itself. Ask the children to explore the mathematical systems used in other civilisations such as Rome, Ancient Greece and Ancient Egypt.

Benin

Benin is still a modern-day society which is situated to the west of Nigeria and east of Togo. It used to be a major West African state although it only became known to the outside world during the period of European expansionism in the seventeenth century.

There is evidence that Benin was first established as a kingship around 1000AD. Prior to that, the society had been ruled by a number of dynasties. However, by the end of the thirteenth century it is believed that these had collapsed and the ruler sent a message to the ruler of the Oba Kingdom asking for someone to rule over Benin. A ruler was duly sent and the Obas, throughout this period,

became enormously important, but there is little evidence that they ruled in a violent or arbitrary manner. They tended to rule through chiefs and sub-chiefs, who complemented each other's powers and placed limits on what the Oba could do. Eventually, the ruler of Benin became known as the Oba Ewuare. One of the most successful Oba Ewuares reigned from around 1440. He added over 200 towns to those already under the control of his people.

By 1600 a Dutchman called Dierick Ruiters had been to Benin. His reports suggested that Benin was a broad and spacious city with a luxurious palace for the king. He also reported on an annual ritual called 'the public progress', when the king went round the exterior of his palace riding a decorated horse and followed by over 400 men, horses and musicians.

It is important to stress that Benin was a stable and well-ordered society. Dutch traders often reported how civil the people were. However, there were elements of it that were unfamiliar to the European visitors who came in increasing numbers after 1600. (For example, the Oba had 1,000 wives.) In addition to Dutch traders, relationships were also established with Portugal, which made a significant missionary initiative in to Benin and the societies of Portugal and Benin exchanged ambassadors.

There is ample archaeological evidence from Benin even today. There are many pieces of ornate jewellery, stone statues and other artefacts and there are many paintings and diaries made by the Dutch who spent much time in Benin during the seventeenth century.

Teaching plan

A series of activities on the Benin could be organised as follows.
• The role of the kings of Benin and their relationship with the chiefs.
• The palace.
• The people and culture of Benin.
• Benin's relations with the wider world.
• Benin's religion.

ACTIVITIES

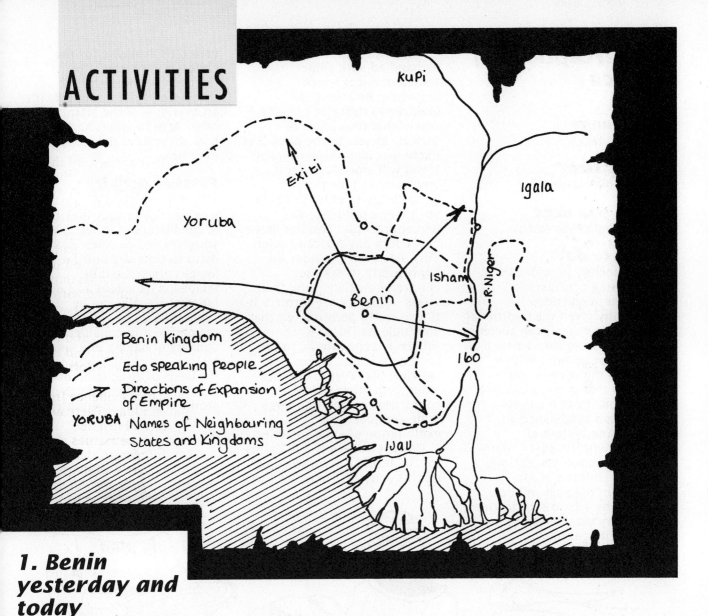

Map labels: kuPi, Exiti, Yoruba, Igala, Isham, R. Niger, Benin, 160, Iuav

Legend:
- Benin kingdom
- Edo speaking people
- Directions of Expansion of Empire
- YORUBA Names of Neighbouring States and Kingdoms

1. Benin yesterday and today

Age range
Nine to eleven.

Group size
Individuals.

What you need
Atlases showing West Africa in the seventeenth and twentieth centuries.

What to do
Benin still exists as a modern-day society and it is a useful exercise for the children to use atlases to find out whether the geographical boundaries of this country have changed over time. This also gives the children experience in using a gazetteer and they may well be able to find some basic information about Benin today. They could also suggest ways in which they might find out more about Benin today and see how far anything they discover highlights important elements of Benin history.

Ask the children to draw two maps comparing seventeenth-century Benin with Benin today and in particular who its neighbours were then and today. They could also find out which European country ruled the other West African states. The children may notice that names of some of the states have changed and they should try to find out both the original colonial name of West African societies and their modern names. When did these states gain independence?

2. Perceptions of Africa

Age range
Nine to eleven.

Group size
The whole class.

What you need
No special requirements.

What to do
Benin society provides an interesting contrast for children to consider, especially given the traditional perceptions of African society. It is clear from the evidence of the Europeans who visited Benin in the seventeenth century that it was a civilised and sophisticated society which had established an interesting system of government. However, many of the common perceptions held by children of African society in the past will be shaped by a Euro-centric view of history established in the nineteenth century.

Although this issue has to be handled with some sensitivity, it is worth beginning by asking the children to describe or write down what they know of African society in the past. It is likely that many stereotypical views will emerge and it is important to take the opportunity to point out how such views influence the perceptions that children have of modern day African society. This, however, provides an opportunity to ask the children how they think their views of history are formed. It is also worth pointing out that although the Dutch were relatively sympathetic to the society of Benin, it was also the case that eventually they, along with other European countries, entered into large scale conquest and exploitation of such societies.

However, there is a dilemma for the teacher when working on this activity. There are few materials available for the children to research for themselves and so it is therefore useful if you provide an overview of the history of other African states and show how these have developed over time.

Further activity
The children should consider what sort of images they have of the history of other societies and peoples. Ask them to consider how far these images are created by television or videos and how far they actually can be substantiated by the *facts*. Ask the children to consider the dangers of having one view of history, which may well form the basis of an opinion or prejudice against a particular group of people or country.

CHAPTER 12

Assessing the National Curriculum

Not surprisingly, since the introduction of the more formal assessment arrangements of the National Curriculum, teachers have been very concerned to ensure that their pupils achieve the appropriate levels at the end of the different key stages. In one sense this has been a valuable aid to learning and teaching, as it has focused attention on the outcomes rather than just the processes. In particular, in history it is a way of ensuring that the children's knowledge and skills are developed in a coherent and rational way, especially in light of the evidence that, in the past, children's access to historical knowledge and understanding tended to be very haphazard. The danger is, however, that teachers become so obsessed with the statements of attainment that they lose sight of the essential teaching and learning that must take place if children are to achieve their targets. It is important to remember that the most constructive assessment takes place on a daily, or even, it could be said, a minute by minute basis, as teachers' judge how far pupils have learned what they have been taught. This process is no different for history, although traditionally teachers tended not to look in the same detail at pupils' learning here as they would have in areas such as English and mathematics. Clearly, teachers will be using the judgements they make to measure children's progress against the different statements of attainment across the three attainment targets.

BACKGROUND

Assessing progress in history

So how can we assess children's progress in history? Inevitably, there is a knowledge-based component and this is often best tested by asking children questions as the topic progresses, on a day to day basis. Progress can be checked again at key points during the topic, for example at the end of a week's lessons. This is best done with individuals or small groups, encouraging the children to give more than a one word response, explaining what they know in more detail. Children can also be assessed in history as they work, demonstrating how they handle evidence or make judgements based on artefacts. History, like many other areas of the National Curriculum, demands that children work in some detail and therefore finished pieces of work need to be assessed for the level of depth and understanding which they exhibit.

Perhaps the most neglected area of assessment is where pupils are allowed to ask themselves questions about what they have learned and how this learning is specifically related to history. Photocopiable page 191 is intended to provide a pupil's own assessment sheet, which seeks to draw together some of the main threads across the three attainment targets. Essentially, this is the pupil's own record of achievement and allows him to think about the different knowledge, skills and attitudes which he has acquired across the study of a particular period of history.

Photocopiable page 192 is intended to provide a more formal record of the progress of a pupil across each of the areas outlined in the three attainment targets.

So when do we know when a child has achieved an appropriate standard that would allow the teacher to say of her, with confidence, that she has achieved a particular statement of attainment? When attainment targets and each of their statements of attainment are studied, it is clear that there will be different levels of achievement necessary for different statements of attainment. For example, under Attainment Target 1: 'Knowledge and understanding of history', Level 3b requires that pupils should be able to 'give a reason for an historical event or development'. The example cited is that a pupil should be able to 'select from a list of possible causes one reason why, in Victorian times, the railways became a more important form of transport than canals'. It could be argued that if a pupil answers this question correctly once, a teacher is then entitled to say that he has been able to give a reason for an historical event or development. This is somewhat simplistic and the teacher would wish, perhaps, to give the child an opportunity to demonstrate this ability in a number of contexts before realistically saying that he could give a reason for an historical event or development.

However, if you look at Level 3 from Attainment Target 3: 'The use of historical sources', where pupils should be able to 'make deductions from historical sources', this suggests that the children have to be able to identify more than just single causes for historical events. Clearly, this envisages a child being able to make a number of observations and deductions, based on evidence and artefacts.

Therefore, teachers need to become familiar with the different statements of attainment at different levels and, over time, in order to develop their own view of when they would confidently say that a pupil is able to do something at a particular stage.

Using the results of assessment

So how should we make use of the information that is gathered from assessment? The National Curriculum envisages a key role for the provision of information to other interested parties, particularly parents. There is an assumption that parents would be most interested in a formal statement of the different levels of achievement that their children have achieved. This is unlikely to be the case if for no other reason than parents are unlikely to understand what achievement at different levels of the National Curriculum for history actually means. Therefore, although it is important to have this information available to parents, it is likely to be more useful to give a brief summary and description of how children have progressed in their knowledge of and development in history and their use of their skills of history. Don't forget, of course, to allow the children themselves to share with their parents what they have found out about history. The chart supplied on photocopiable page 191 will give children a useful basis from which to discuss their progress in history with their parents.

Assessment and its results are also useful to other teachers as they plan the next programme of work. Clearly, this has to be in the context of the school's overall plan for teaching historical study units both at Key Stage 1 and Key Stage 2. However, carefully kept records should allow a teacher to provide the best possible support and set realistic targets for children.

The most powerful use of assessment is when a teacher uses it to provide the next appropriate opportunity for a child in the class. To give a specific example, if a child has achieved Level 3 of Attainment Target 3: 'The use of historical sources' and has demonstrated that she can make deductions from historical sources, the teacher should be sensitive to allow that child to then draw information from different historical sources in a period, thus allowing the child to achieve Level 4 of Attainment Target 3.

A T CHART

England and Wales

The chart on this page refers to the National Curriculum for England and Wales. Use this chart to identify the attainment targets covered by the activities in this book. Activities are identified by their chapter number which is in bold, section (ordered alphabetically as they occur in the chapter), and activity numbers; for example, **11**/d1 means Chapter 11, Indus Valley section (being the fourth section), Activity 1.

AT / Level	1 Knowledge and understanding of history	2 Interpretations of history	3 The use of historical sources
1	**1**/1,3, **7**/8 **9**/5	**1**/2,4,10 **2**/4 **7**/4	**1**/5,6,8-10
2	**1**/2,5,6,9,10 **2**/1,2,5 **3**/a1	**1**/7,8,10 **2**/4,7,8	**1**/2,5,8-10 **2**/1-3,5,8
3	**2**/1,3,5,7 **3**/a1 **4**/6,9 **5**/3,8,10 **6**/4,8 **7**/2,3 **8**/7 **9**/a2,5/b2,4,6/c2,3,5/d2-5/e1,2/f2-4 **10**/a1,2/b1,2/,c1 **11**/b1	**2**/6-8 **3**/a2/b1,2 **4**/5 **5**/7,9 **6**/5 **9**/a3/b1,3,4,6/c2/d3,4 **10**/a1/b1,2 **11**/a3	**1**/9 **2**/1-3,6,8 **3**/a2,4/b1,2 **4**/4-6,8 **5**/1,3 **6**/1,2,4,5,9 **7**/3,4,7 **8**/1,3,4 **9**/a2/c1/d2,4,5/e3,4/f3,4 **10**/a1,2/
4	**3**/a3,4/b1-3/c3 **4**/1,2,4,7,9 **5**/3,4,6-10 **6**/1-4,6-8 **7**/1-5,7,9 **8**/1-7 **9**/a1,2,4-6/b2-4,6/c2,3,5/d1-5/e1-3,5/f1-4 **10**/a1,2/b1,2/c1 **11**/a1,3/b3/c1-3/d1,3/e1,2/f1	**3**a2,4/b1,2/c1-3 **4**/3,5,8 **5**/2-4,6,7,9,10 **6**/3,5,9 **7**/3,4,6,8,9 **8**/1,6 **9**/a3,5/	**3**/a1,2,4/b1-3/c1-3 **4**/2,3,5,8 **5**/1,3-8 **6**/1-5,7-9 **7**/3,4,7 **8**/1-3 **9**/a1-3,5/b1-4,6/c1-4/d2,4,5/e4,5/f2-4 **10**/a1,2/b1,2/c1
5	**3**/a4/c2,3 **4**/7,9 **5**/3,6,8,10 **6**/2-4,7,8 **7**/3,7 **8**/2 **9**/a2,4/b2-4,6/c2,5/d2,3/e3 **10**/a1,2/b1,2/c1 **11**/b3,c1-3/d3/f1	**3**/a1,2/b2/c1,2 **4**/3-5 **5**/2,7,9 **6**/5,7 **7**/3,9 **8**/3 **9**/a3/b1,3,4,6/c2,5/d3/e3,5/f2,4 **10**/a1,2/b1,2	**3**/a1,2,4/b2 **4**/5,9 **5**/1,7 **6**/2,5-7 **7**/3,4,8 **9**/a3/b1-4,6/c2,4/e5/f4 **11**/d2,3

CHAPTER 13

Other issues

Links with other subjects

Although history is identified as a separate subject within the National Curriculum, there is no requirement that it be taught exclusively on its own. Careful planning will allow teachers to cover a range of other subjects within the context of a history topic. A traditional topic web is a useful way of planning and, before a topic begins, it is worthwhile brainstorming a number of ideas under each of the other curriculum areas. The following is an example using Core study unit 4, Britain since 1930.

English
Writing diary accounts of evacuation during the Second World War.
Holding a debate about the good things and the bad things to have emerged from the 1960s.
Reading children's fiction.

Mathematics
The cost of living in 1930, 1950 and 1990.
Decimalisation.
Imperial and metric measures.
Using a ration book.

Technology
The impact of computer technology on British industry.
Advertising and design in the 1960s.
Evaluating council house architecture in the post-war period.

Religious education
Changes in patterns of worship.
Places of worship.
The incidences of other religions during the period.

Britain since 1930

Art
'Pop' art from the 1960s.
Changes in fashion since 1930.

Science
The effects of pollution on British society, particularly in the last 20 or 30 years.
Scientific advances since 1930.

Music
Changes in the popular styles of music, such as rock and roll, classical, jazz, soul and pop.

Geography
Compare industrial, social and economic patterns of distribution between the early part of this period and later part of the period.
Describe population changes during the period.
Examine transport links during the period.

Cross-curricular themes

Within the National Curriculum, there are a number of cross-curricular themes which have been identified. It is intended that, included in the delivery of each of the individual subjects, opportunities will be taken for references to each of these cross-curricular themes. The history curriculum offers a number of opportunities under each of the themes. The first theme is citizenship. The major elements of citizenship are work, employment and leisure, family, and the nature of community. Each of these elements is likely to be included in almost all of the core study units. For example, in the core study unit 'Victorian Britain' it is possible to identify changing patterns of work due to industrialisation; the extent to which people began to take leisure more seriously and had opportunities to undertake holidays and other entertainments. Patterns of family life during this period could also be examined, as could the change of political dimension which saw the franchise being extended to more people. The supplementary study units 'Food and farming' and 'Domestic life, families and childhood' offer clear opportunities for tracking these three themes over a longer historical period.

The next cross-curricular theme is environmental education. It is possible to see how a theme such as 'Tudor and Stuart times' would allow for a close examination of changing patterns of population brought about by changes in farming methods during the period. Or, children could investigate the negative effects of exploration led by European settlers during the period from 1450 onwards.

Another history-related study might involve pupils examining the changes in landscapes and the effect of human action in making their environment either less or more attractive over a period of years.

The third theme is education and economic and industrial understanding. Almost all of the study units will offer opportunities to study this in more detail. The very first core study unit in Key Stage 2, 'Invaders and settlers', would allow children to examine the economic dimensions of the invasions of the, Romans, Anglo-Saxons and Vikings into Britain. The other studies referring to British history, such as 'Tudor and Stuart times', 'Victorian Britain' and 'Britain since 1930', all require a study of economic and industrial conditions as factors, in order that they may be understood more fully. Look too at ancient civilisations, such as Greece, Assyria and Mesopotamia, in order that children can understand that an economic dimension is important in all human societies. Clearly, the Category A Supplementary study units such as 'Ships and seafarers', 'Food and farming' and 'Land transport' are all intimately related to the development of economic prosperity over time.

The next cross-curricular theme is health education. The children can examine different periods in history and compare and contrast the living conditions of the population. An obvious example would be from the Tudor and Stuart times and the effects of the plague. The children can examine the extent to which society has increasingly examined the conditions under which people lived and took steps to alleviate such insanitary conditions. The supplementary study unit on 'Food and farming' could also be used to track different patterns of eating habits throughout time and how society, even in the last 10 or 15 years, has significantly changed its attitudes to healthy eating.

The final cross-curricular theme is careers education and guidance. Here history is important in allowing the children to learn about a wide range of adult occupations. It should also allow them to see how some occupations have evolved and even disappeared over time as other occupations and opportunities have taken place.

The National Curriculum has also identified cross-curricular skills which can be developed in all subjects. These would include communication,

numeracy, problem-solving, information handling and study skills. It is obvious that each of these can be exercised in any study unit. For example, children will need to communicate their historical findings in a variety of ways. This could include writing, setting up displays of artefacts, the use of themes and the use of information technology. Children can also handle many problems in history by asking themselves questions about the choices and decisions that different people have made in different historical periods.

Information technology

In all subjects of the National Curriculum children are expected to develop an information technology capability. Information technology can help with historical enquiry, as well as communicating the results of the children's historical studies. For example, children can develop their own databases on subjects such as occupations in the past, or they can use customised packages referring to census returns. Children can also communicate using their historical findings through graphs, diagrams, as well as using word-processing facilities, to present their information in an interesting and exciting way.

Equal opportunities

Historical study inevitably requires examination of the different roles of men and women throughout time. Children should be encouraged to examine how far historical developments and periods have largely excluded women from playing a significant part in history. The children can consider why and how the twentieth century has seen such a significant change in the role and position of women. In addition, the children should be encouraged to look at historical sources for evidence of bias or evidence of a single perspective. For example, how many diary entries are written by men?

A multicultural dimension can also be introduced through studies of different periods of British history and, in particular, the contribution made by new immigrants to Britain in the period since 1930. The first core study unit of Key Stage 2, 'Invaders and settlers', allows children to understand that the history of Britain has largely been about the arrival of newcomers and the assimilation of such people into the life and culture of the country. It is important to avoid using history to moralise, but children need to be aware of natural patterns of development, such as emigration and immigration, in order that they understand that society does not stand still but evolves through time.

Meeting specific needs

The vast majority of history teaching in a primary school is likely to involve mixed-ability classes or groups or individuals working on tasks given to the whole class. There is evidence from several HMI studies that teachers who would otherwise differentiate work in curricular areas such as science, maths and English tend not to do the same for history. There are some advantages in this, in that teachers would argue that many examining such as working evidence and handling artefacts involves significant exchange of ideas and discussion. These teachers would further say that such discussions encourage all children, of whatever abilities, to make a valid and valuable contribution. The danger is, however, that historical work is given to children which far exceeds their abilities. In particular, when children are asked to handle firsthand evidence or even secondary sources, there is an expectation that they will be able to read and understand sometimes complex language. Therefore teachers need to show sensitivity in ensuring that their pupils have access to the whole range of work in history, but that they are not then excluded from certain areas on the grounds that the tasks they are set are inappropriate. Artefacts, photographs, newspapers and so on, offer children of all abilities the opportunity to handle the past at firsthand.

The children who are less proficient at communicating their findings in writing, can make use of facilities such as tape recorders, which allow them to express their feelings and findings in a way which is not inhibiting. One significant advantage of history is that children who might not succeed in other areas of the curriculum, can often take a particular interest in finding out about the past. Such children can often far exceed the expectations that teachers have of them.

History also offers opportunities for the most able children in a class to be stretched to their full potential. In particular, it allows such children to look at causes and consequences and have them consider why people in historical situations acted in the ways that they did. The skill of the historian is to see the past through the eyes of the people who lived in an historical period and not through the eyes of the twentieth century. Encourage the children to use as much evidence as possible to build up a picture of a period in the past and use that evidence and information to make informed judgements about why people behaved in the way that they did.

CHAPTER 14

Resources for teaching history

With the choice of historical topics being circumscribed by the National Curriculum, schools are likely to be able to develop resource banks covering each of the study units. This is the most efficient way of ensuring that teachers provide each other with support over a number of years. So, for example, if a teacher has been working on Core study unit 2 'Tudor and Stuart times', he should keep together plans, worksheets, posters, teacher guides and so on, which have been used and found useful. These should then be stored in a central resource bay within the school from which other teachers can draw upon when they come to teach the same unit.

Books

Not surprisingly, books as secondary sources are going to be the most important resource. Schools will need to make intelligent choices about which titles and in what quantity they purchase books. In particular this will require the person responsible for co-ordinating history teaching to keep up to date with new materials. Schools should also consider using central resources such as the school library service or other library provision. Where such services are available, schools can build up their own core collection of books while at the same time have access to a large number of books on a particular topic.

Although a wide range of new resources is available to support the teaching of history, suitable books for this study unit are still quite scarce. However, the Encyclopedia Britannica provides excellent background information.

Story books

Story books are a useful supplement to a school's resources. They can be used:
• to help children understand new concepts and develop historical skills;
• to promote children's understanding and use of historical vocabulary;
• to develop an understanding of life in particular historical periods.
• to explore the motives, feelings and characters of people in history.

Other printed resources

Schools, themselves, are likely to have their own resources which can prove helpful when teaching history. Therefore an important job for the history co-ordinator is to act as a school's archivist. It is very tempting to allow old registers, photographs and books to gather dust in the stock cupboard, but it is important that these are recognised both as a curriculum resource for the future and as an important source of evidence about the life and work of the school. Over time, it might be possible for the school to build up its own collection of census returns, parish registers, log books and so on.

Other written resources which can be collected include newspapers and magazines. A number of facsimile newspapers relating to different periods or important events in history are now available and these are extremely useful. Other useful materials would include such things as postcards, posters, programmes and tickets.

Artefacts

Any study of an historical period is likely to be enhanced by children having access to a variety of artefacts, such as household objects, coins, toys and so on. These could also include clothes, both original and copies of originals. It is important that the school builds up its own collection over a period of time and perhaps establishes somewhere in the school where these items are displayed and changed at frequent intervals.

Educational broadcasts and other audio resources

There are now some excellent schools television broadcasts such as *Zig Zag* (BBC) and *How we used to live* (Yorkshire) which provide valuable support for history topics. It is important, however, that these are used intelligently because the teaching of history consists of much more than allowing the children to watch television! Build up your own video library of such programmes, along with other videos relating to particular years or periods.

Museums, art galleries and libraries

All of these places provide valuable support to schools. Keep in touch with your local museum service and ask them for help on particular topics. Many museums and art galleries now inform schools of projected exhibitions and very often will relate exhibitions to particular forthcoming educational broadcasts.

Human resources

Human resources are often the most neglected, but probably the most valuable, of all resources. People themselves are an excellent source of historical knowledge, and any study which involves events in the recent, or not so recent, past could make use of these eyewitnesses and experts. Invite people into school and ask them to share their memories with the children and record the interviews to be stored and used again and again. Don't forget too, to involve parents and families as they can provide information or artefacts relevant to topics or bring specialist knowledge or skills into school.

Useful addresses

The Historical Association, 59a Kennington Park Road, London SE11 4JH, Tel. 071 735 3901 (Primary membership available) – *History* (4 issues), *Teaching History* (12 issues).
Association for History and Computing, c/o Editor Department of Economic and Social History, William Robertson Building, George Square, Edinburgh EH8 9JH.
The Folklore Society, University College London, Gower Street, London WC1E 6BT, Tel. 071 387 7050 (The Children's Folklore Group is a specialist section within the Society).
The National Trust, 36 Queen Anne's Gate, London SW1H 9AS, Tel. 071 222 9251.
English Heritage Education Centre, Key Sign House, 429 Oxford Street, London W1R 2HD, Tel. 071 973 3442/3.
Oral History Society & Journal, c/o The National Sound Archive, 29 Exhibition Road, London SW7 2AS.

History and information technology

ICSA (ESM) for 8–13 year-olds; concerning Roman Britain.

Digging Deeper into History (English Heritage) – Key Stages 2, 3 and GCSE.

Into the Unknown (Tressell) for 10–14 year-olds; concerning a 15th Century voyage.

PHOTOCOPIABLES

The pages in this section can be photocopied and adapted to suit your own needs and those of your class; they do not need to be declared in respect of any photocopying licence. Each photocopiable page relates to a specific activity in the main body of the book and the appropriate activity and page references are given above each photocopiable sheet.

Farming and food rhymes, page 95

Miller-dee, miller-dee, dusty poll
How many sacks of flour hast thou stole!
In goes a bushel, out comes a peck
Hang old miller-dee up by the neck.

This comes from the seventeenth century when farmers complained that the millers kept back too much flour for themselves.

A day in the life of..., page 16

...ees in May,
...d of hay;
...ees in June,
...er spoon;
...es in July,
...y.

...when beekeepers
...arly summer.

...ne for the sparrow
...ne for the crow
...ne to rot
...d one to grow.

...teenth or seventeenth century
...imes the number of seeds

Patterns of employment, page 69

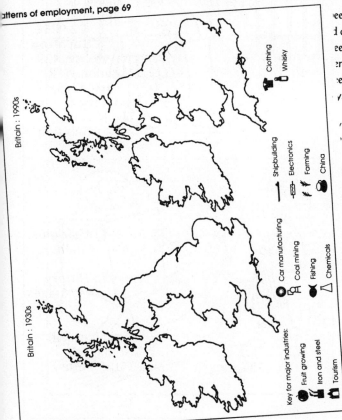

Britain : 1990s

Britain : 1930s

Key for major industries:

Clothing
Whisky
Shipbuilding
Electronics
Farming
China
Car manufacturing
Coal mining
Fishing
Chemicals
Fruit growing
Iron and steel
Tourism

Cars, cars, cars, page 27

1940s

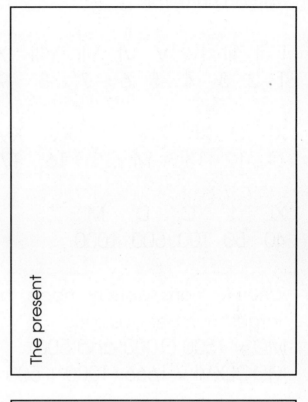

The present

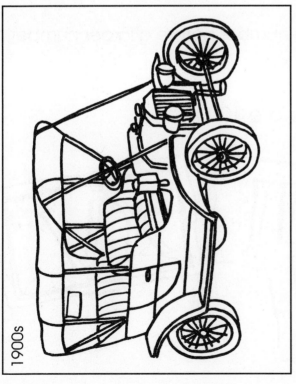

1900s

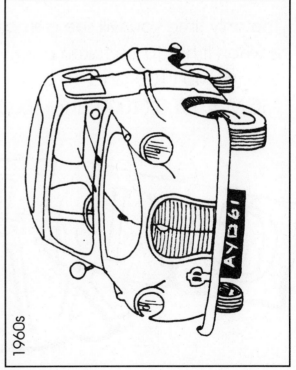

1960s

Roman numerals

I II III IV V VI VII VIII IX X
1 2 3 4 5 6 7 8 9 10

XI XII XIII XIV XV XVI XVI XVIII XIX XX
11 12 13 14 15 16 17 18 19 20

XL L C D M
40 50 100 500 1000

When Romans wrote numbers, they put them in order so that the largest number was first.
MD = 1500 (1000 and 500)
MDCLXVI = 1666 (1000 + 500 + 100 + 50 + 10 + 5 + 1)

The only time you will see a smaller number before a larger number is when it has to be taken away.
CXL = 140 (100 and 10 before 50)
MCM = 1900 (1000 and 100 before 1000)

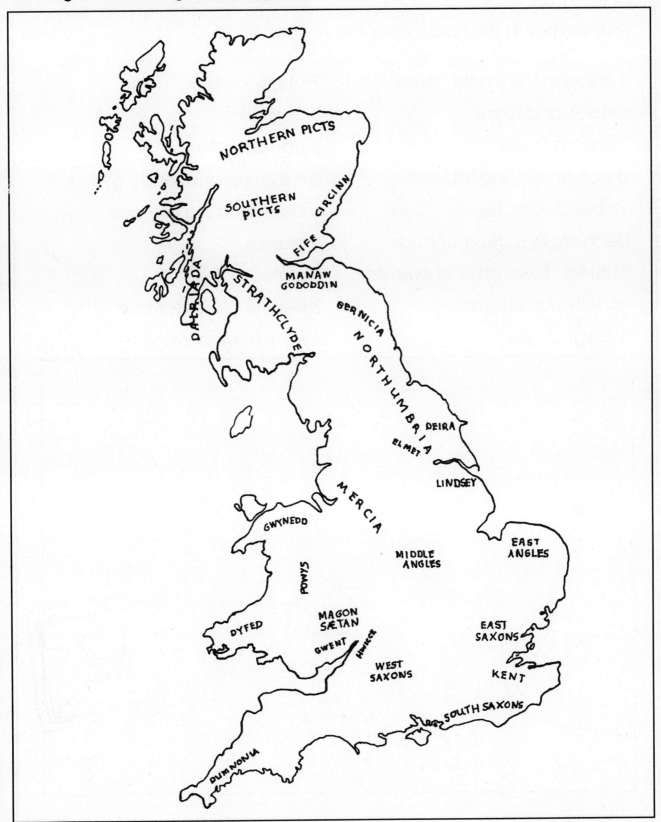

The furniture in the house of Sir Henry Parker *c.*1570.

2 chairs in the whole house	7 cupboards
8 stools and forms	3 carpets
2 square tables	3 candlesticks
a pair of 'playing tables'	fire shovels and tongs
12 bedsteads, tapestry and bedhangings, feather beds, bolsters, blankets and cushions of velvet and satin	a basin and jug of water
	6 glasses
	6 plates for fruit
	2 pewter plates for tarts
3 great chests	1 stool of black velvet

Extracts from Samuel Pepys's diary

In 1665, Pepys wrote this in his diary:

June 7th 1665:   This day I did in Drury Lane see two or three houses marked
with a red cross upon the doors and 'Lord have mercy upon
us' writ there which was a sad sight to me.

June 21st 1665:   I find all the town almost going out of town, the coaches and
wagons being all full of people going into the country.

And, in 1666, Pepys wrote about the fire:

September 2nd 1666: Jane called us up about 3 in the morning, to tell us of a
great fire they saw in the City.

day	month ＿＿＿＿＿＿＿＿ year 19＿＿＿＿	

'... no shirt and no waistcoat; all his neck and a great part of his chest being bare. A ragged cloth jacket hung about him, and was tied, so as to keep it together, with bits of tape. What he had wrapped round for his trousers did not cover one of his legs while one of his thighs was bare. He wore two old shoes: one tied to his foot with an old ribbon, the other a woman's old boot. He had an old cloth cap. His features were distorted somewhat through being swollen with the cold.'

From 'London Labour and the London Poor' by Henry Mayhew (1861), reprinted by Dover Publications, 1968.

School fees, 1876

'3d per week per child, except when more than two in the family attend, when a reduction of 1d per week would be made after the first child, thus one child 3d per week, two ditto 6d, three ditto 7d, four ditto 9d, and so on. Five hours in each day would actually be devoted to instruction with an interval of a few minutes for recreation.'

'The Beckenham Journal', November 1876

Conversion table

1p = 2.4d (2.4 old pence)

5p = 1s (shilling)

50p = 10s (10 shillings)

£1 = £1

12d = 1 shilling

20 shillings = £1

£1.05 = 21 shillings (a guinea)

Weekly income of the family

	£ s d	£ s d
Nominal weekly wages of man	0 16 0	
Perquisites	0 2 0	
Actual weekly wages of man		0 18 0
Nominal weekly wages of wife	6	
Perquisites in coal and wood	1 4	
Actual weekly wages of wife		0 7 4
Nominal weekly wages of boy		0 3 0
Total income		1 8 4

Weekly expenditure of the family

	£ s d		£ s d		£ s d
Rent	0 3 0	Beer (home)	0 2 0	Clothes	0 2 0
Candle	0 0 3 1/2	Beer (work)	0 1 6	Boots and shoes	0 1 6
Bread	0 2 1	Spirits	0 1 0	Milk	0 0 7
Butter	0 0 10	Cheese	0 0 6	Salt and pepper	0 0 1
Sugar	0 0 8	Flour	0 0 3	Tobacco	0 0 9
Tea	0 0 10	Suet	0 0 3	Wear and tear of	
Coffee	0 0 4	Fruit	0 0 3	bedding, crocks, etc.	0 0 3
Butcher's		Rice	0 0 0 1/2	Schooling for girl	0 0 3
meat	3 6	Soap	0 0 6	Baking Sunday's	
Bacon	0 1 2	Starch	0 0 0 1/2	dinner	0 0 2
Potatoes	0 0 10	Soda and		Mangling	0 0 3
Raw fish	0 0 4	blue	0 0 1	Amusements	
Herrings	0 0 4	Dubbing	0 0 0 1/2	and sundries	0 1 0
					1 7 6

From *London Labour and the London Poor* (1861) by Henry Mayhew, reprinted by Dover Publications, 1968.

Parents' time, page 66

A questionnaire for someone at home

I interviewed (name) _____

In what year did you become a teenager? _____

Where did you live? _____

What school did you go to? _____

What was your favourite pop group and why? _____

_____

_____

_____

What clothes did you wear:

• to school? _____

• to special events or to parties? _____

_____

What were your favourite television programmes? _____

_____

Did you have a favourite film? _____

How much pocket money did you get? _____

What news items do you remember as a teenager? _____

_____

_____

Write down your memories of being a teenager. _____

_____

_____

_____

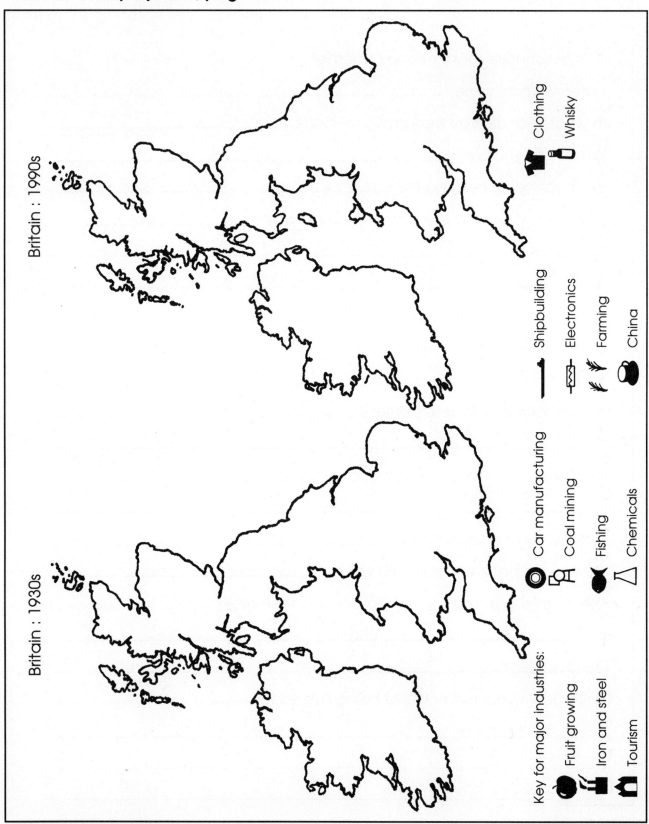

Britain : 1990s

Britain : 1930s

Key for major industries:

Car manufacturing

Coal mining

Fishing

Chemicals

Shipbuilding

Electronics

Farming

China

Fruit growing

Iron and steel

Tourism

Clothing

Whisky

The Greek alphabet, page 77

Greek letter	name of letter	English sound
α	alpha	a
β	beta	b
γ	gamma	g
δ	delta	d
ε	epsilon	e
ζ	zeta	z
η	eta	e
θ	theta	th
ι	iota	i
κ	kappa	k
λ	lambda	l
μ	mu	m
ν	nu	n
μ	xi	x/ks
ο	omicron	o
π	pi	p
ρ	rho	r
σ/ξ	sigma	s
τ	tau	t
υ	upsilon	u
φ	phi	f/ph
χ	chi	ch
ψ	psi	ps
ω	omega	o

What do you think these Greek words mean in English? You could guess first and then look up what you think the word is in English. A good dictionary should tell you what the origin of the word is.

polis   demos   podium   stadium

These English words have Greek origins. Use a dictionary to find out which parts of the words are Greek and what they mean.

pentagon   democracy   delta
philosophy   Eureka   alphabet
phobia   telescope   arithmatic
thermometer   pantechnicon

Time frame, page 78

	Greece	Europe	Asia	Africa
2000BC	c.2000–1700 Greek speaking people arrive in Greece.			
1500BC	c.1600–1200 Mycenaean civilisation develops in Mycenae and Tiryns. c.1450 Cretan civillisation destroyed.			
1000BC	c.1200–800 Collapse of Mycenaen civilisation.			
500BC	c.850 Homer writes the *Iliad* and the *Odyssey*. c.850–650 Rise of the City States. c.580 Beginning of Athenian democracy. c.490–479 Persians defeated at Marathon, win at Thermopylae, lose at Salaniis.			
AD1	431 Peloponnesian War. 334–327 Alexander establishes empire from Egypt to India.			

The ship below is the *Santa Maria*. Can you draw the following on to the outline?

- Columbus's cabin
- helm
- compass
- cannon

- pump to draw water from the hold
- windlass to operate sails and anchor
- hold with provisions, for example water, wine, beef, sardines, flour and garlic

- store for sails
- arms and gunpowder
- ropes and hawsers

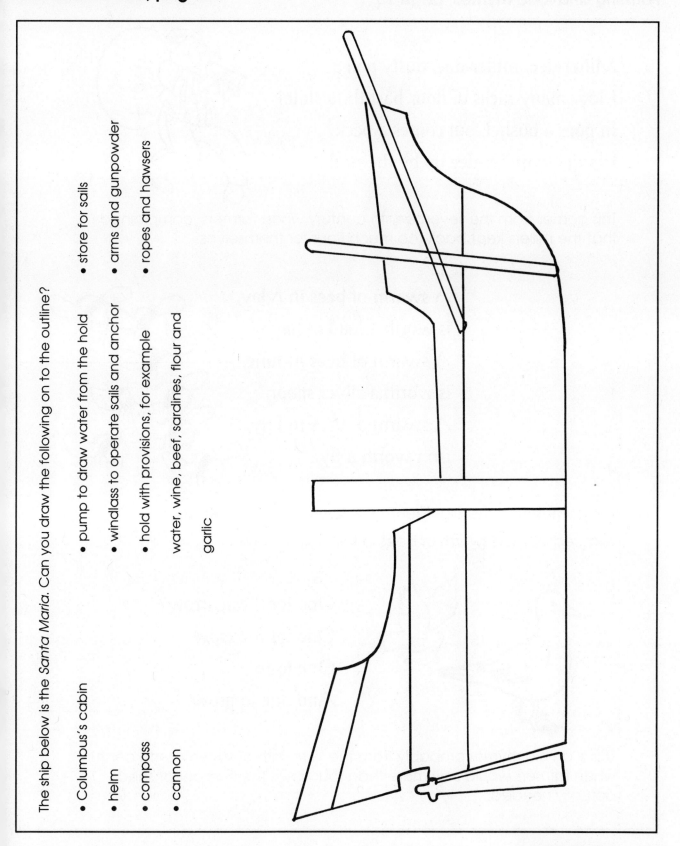

Miller-dee, miller-dee, dusty poll
How many sacks of flour hast thou stole?
In goes a bushel, out comes a peck
Hang old miller-dee up by the neck.

This comes from the seventeenth century when farmers complained that the millers kept back too much flour for themselves.

A swarm of bees in May,
is worth a load of hay;
A swarm of bees in June,
is worth a silver spoon;
A swarm of bees in July,
isn't worth a fly.

This comes from the eighteenth century when beekeepers wanted a good swarm of bees in the early summer.

One for the sparrow
One for the crow
One to rot
And one to grow.

This is an old rhyme, probably from the sixteenth or seventeenth century when farmers would sow more than four times the number of seeds actually needed.

Stained-glass windows, page 101

Find these cathedrals and mark them on the map by drawing a cathedral symbol in the appropriate place.

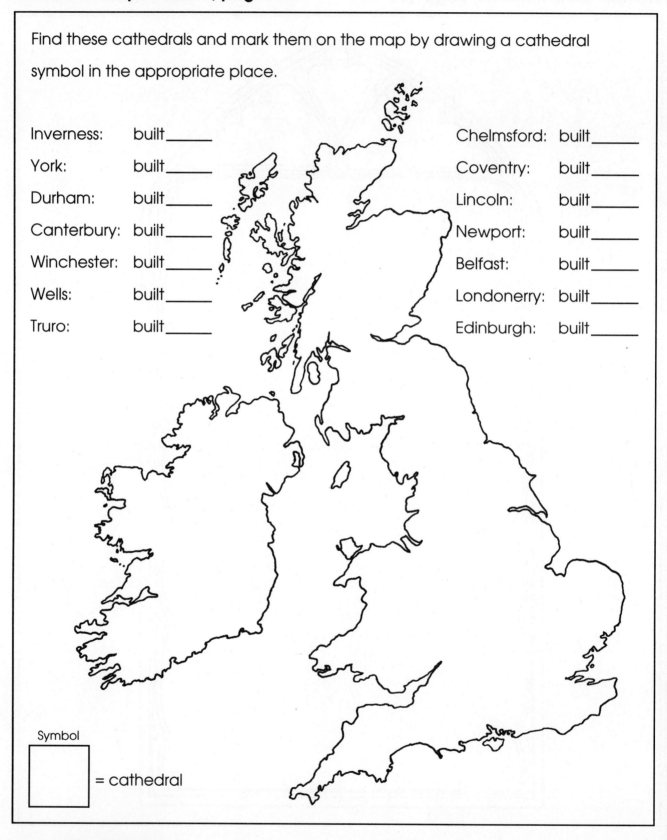

Inverness:	built_____		Chelmsford:	built_____
York:	built_____		Coventry:	built_____
Durham:	built_____		Lincoln:	built_____
Canterbury:	built_____		Newport:	built_____
Winchester:	built_____		Belfast:	built_____
Wells:	built_____		Londonerry:	built_____
Truro:	built_____		Edinburgh:	built_____

Symbol

☐ = cathedral

Here is an example of a piece of illuminated manuscript.

The lord's my shepherd i shall not want psalm 23

Can you do a piece of writing in such a style?

Can you do the same piece of writing using a modern script from

a word processor? Attach the computer print-out here.

Finally, can you write the piece in your own handwriting?

OXFORD One day Stage-Coach

These are to give Notice to all Persons that have occasion to go to Oxford by Coach; Let them repair to the Greyhound in Holborn, where they may be furnished with a good Coach and able Horses, which sets forth every Monday, Wednesday, and Friday for Oxford, performing the Stage in one day; and sets forth from the Mitre in Oxford for London, every Tuesday, Thursday, and Saturday; performed if God permit, By

    Widow STONEHILL
    JOHN FOSSET

The Stage begins Munday next, being the 17th instant April, and sets forth precisely at Six in the morning.

A JOURNEY FROM OXFORD

Life in Ur
• Streets: unpaved, narrow, no mules allowed in them.
• Rooms: small lobby with a jar of water for washing. Main rooms built around a central court, open to the sky.
• Guest room, slaves quarters, storerooms, lavatory and kitchen all on the lower floor.
• Houses: no lower windows, small upper windows with reed lattices.
• Furnishings: stools, low chairs, tables, chests, wicker baskets, cups, bowls, vases.

The Mayan system of counting:

Using the Mayan system, can you solve the following problems?

Set out and solve these problems using the Mayan system:
Ninteen minus three equals?   Eleven and eight equals?
Four and four and four equals?   Twelve and six equals?

Can you use a reference book to find out how Mayan numbers above twenty were written?

My history record sheet, page 156

My history record sheet

Name _____

Topic studied _____

I began this study in _____ and finished it in _____

I consulted these reference books: _____

(list four)   _____

                                   _____

                                   _____

I undertook these visits: _____

_____

Here are my five most interesting facts from this topic:

I've studied these historical documents and sources:

The five key dates in this period were:

I've learned these new words during this study and I've listed what they mean:

My favourite character from this period was:

Here are three things from this period which historians are not so sure about:

Legend:
- ▨ Tested
- ☒ Understood
- ◩ Had experience of

NAME:

Levels	1			2			3			4			5		
Attainment targets	a	b	c	a	b	c	a	b	c	a	b	c	a	b	c
1. KNOWLEDGE AND UNDERSTANDING OF HISTORY															
Comments:															
2. INTERPRETATIONS OF HISTORY															
Comments:															
3. THE USE OF HISTORICAL SOURCES															
Comments:															